Massachusetts

SUPPLEMENT FOR

Modern Real Estate Practice

Consulting Editor

DAVID L. KENT

FIFTH EDITION

Dearborn™

Real Estate Education

This publication is designed to provide accurate and authoritative information in regard to the subject matter covered. It is sold with the understanding that a publisher is not engaged in rendering legal, accounting, or other professional service. If legal advice or other expert assistance is required, the services of a competent professional person should be sought.

Publisher: Carol Luitjens
Senior Real Estate Writer: Evan M. Butterfield, MA, JD
Project Editor: Margaret Haywood

Published by Real Estate Education Company®,
a division of Dearborn Financial Publishing, Inc.®
155 North Wacker Drive
Chicago, Illinois 60606-1719
(312) 836-4400
http://www.real-estate-ed.com

Printed in the United States of America.

10 9 8

Library of Congress Cataloging-in-Publication Data

Massachusetts supplement for Modern real estate practice / consulting
     editor, David L. Kent. — 5th ed.
       p. cm.
    Includes index.
    ISBN 0-7931-1623-6
    1. Real estate business — Law and legislation — Massachusetts.
    2. Vendors and purchasers — Massachusetts. 3. Real property —
    Massachusetts. 4. Real estate business — Massachusetts. I. Kent,
    David L. II. Galaty, Fillmore W. Modern real estate practice.
    KF2042.R4G34 1993 Suppl. 3
    346.74404'37 — dc20   95-40441
    [347.4406437]   CIP

Contents

	Preface	iv
	Preparing for the Real Estate Licensing Examination	v
4	Real Estate Brokerage	1
5	Listing Agreements	12
6	Interests in Real Estate	19
7	How Ownership Is Held	24
8	Legal Descriptions	27
9	Real Estate Taxes and Other Liens	30
10	Real Estate Contracts	33
11	Transfer of Title	46
12	Title Records	52
13	Real Estate License Laws	55
14/15	Real Estate Financing: Principles and Practice	65
16	Leases	67
18	Real Estate Appraisal	71
19/20	Land Use and Development	74
21	Fair Housing Laws and Ethical Practices	77
	Appendix: Environmental Issues and the Real Estate Transaction	81
	Answer Key	91
	Index	93

Preface

The material presented in this book is designed to supplement the text *Modern Real Estate Practice* by Galaty, Allaway and Kyle, also published by Real Estate Education Company, Chicago. The purpose of this *Supplement* is to bring out those facts and practices that <u>materially differ</u> from the main text or that are <u>unique</u> to the real estate business as it is practiced in Massachusetts.

Students should first read the assigned chapter in the main text and then refer to the same chapter in the *Supplement*. For ease of reference, this book follows the overall structure of the main volume. For example, Chapter 5 in this *Supplement* offers Massachusetts-specific information relevant to the general discussion presented in Chapter 5 of *Modern Real Estate Practice*. Students should note that some chapters in the main text have no related chapters in this *Supplement*. Only real estate law or practice issues that are unique to Massachusetts are included for discussion here!

Both Massachusetts-specific and general real estate law and practice are included in the licensing examination! Students need to be thoroughly familiar with the material contained in this *Supplement* <u>and</u> *Modern Real Estate Practice*.

Questions that may be used for both testing and learning follow each chapter. These questions are prepared in a format similar to the Massachusetts Real Estate License Examination. The answer key for the questions is included at the end of this *Supplement*. As you finish each chapter, and before you go on to the next ones, you should be certain that you can answer each question correctly.

CONSULTING EDITOR

Dr. David L. Kent is a professor of business administration at Plymouth State College and a member of the Massachusetts and New Hampshire Bar Associations. Dr. Kent holds an M.B.A. from Northeastern University of Boston and a J.D. from the Boston College Law School. He has been a licensed real estate broker and a real estate consultant for more than 30 years, and has taught real estate law, investment and principles.

Most of the forms used in this text have been provided by the Greater Boston Real Estate Board and the Greater Springfield Association of REALTORS®. All forms are included for illustrative purposes only, and may not be reproduced without the consent of the organization holding the copyright. Special thanks to Noreen A. Nicholson and Ben Scranton for their cooperation.

REVIEWERS

The following people provided invaluable professional guidance in preparing this edition:

- *Shirley R. Slack*, GRI, Carlson Pre-License School

- *Mark P. Higgins, Esq.*, Northeastern University and Carlson Pre-License School

- *Charles A. Bergeron*, Springfield Technical Community College and Manager, Coldwell Banker Keenan Molta Associates

- *Phyllis Rudnick*, GRI, CRS, Annex Real Estate School, Inc.

- *Joseph M. Brice*, MBA, JMB Real Estate Academy, Inc.

- *Mary Ann O'Callaghan*, CRB, CRS, GRI, Better Homes & Gardens

Preparing for the Real Estate
Licensing Examination

In Massachusetts, as in most other states, the real estate profession is regulated. This means that the state of Massachusetts, through the Board of Registration of Real Estate Brokers and Salesmen, has established certain standards for real estate professionals. As a broker or salesperson, you will be expected to be aware of those standards and to comply with them. You are already complying with Massachusetts General Law, Chapter 112, section 87SS by taking an approved pre-license real estate course. Your next step will probably be to take the state licensing exam.

The Massachusetts Real Estate License Examination tests your knowledge of general and state-specific real estate principles and practices — knowledge you will need as a real estate broker or salesperson. Can you locate and identify a property from the legal description on the deed? Can you explain to your client the difference between real estate and personal property? Are you aware of your responsibilities as an agent and of your ethical and legal duties to both buyers and sellers? The Board of Registration needs to determine the extent of your real estate knowledge to find out whether or not you measure up to the standard expected of real estate professionals in Massachusetts.

A general topic guide to the Massachusetts Examination, including the relevant chapters in both this *Supplement* and *Modern Real Estate Practice*, appears at the end of this section.

ABOUT THIS BOOK

The *Modern Real Estate Practice* text presents a solid foundation of basic real estate principles and practices. This book, the *Massachusetts Supplement for Modern Real Estate Practice*, provides additional information about those general principles as they are applied in Massachusetts.

> **Only material relevant to *Massachusetts* real estate practice is included in this book!**

You'll notice that this *Massachusetts Supplement* does not contain as many chapters as *Modern Real Estate Practice*. For example, it begins with Chapter 4, not Chapter 1. That's because it includes only Massachusetts-specific information. If you want a general analysis of easements, read Chapter 6 of *Modern Real Estate Practice*. However, to learn about the specific requirements for an easement in Massachusetts, you should read Chapter 6 of the *Massachusetts Supplement*. If the general information about a particular area contained in *Modern Real Estate Practice* is sufficient for Massachusetts real estate practitioners, there will be little or no discussion of it in the *Massachusetts Supplement*.

By studying both the main text and the *Supplement*, and by working through the tests and exercises included in both books, you should be well prepared for the license examination.

ABOUT THE MASSACHUSETTS REAL ESTATE LICENSE EXAMINATION

The ASI Format

The Massachusetts Real Estate License Examination is prepared and administered by an independent testing service, Assessment Systems, Inc. (ASI), under the supervision of the Massachusetts Board of Real Estate Brokers and Salesmen. ASI offers licensing exams nationwide, but each exam is adapted to local real estate laws and practices and the priorities of the state's licensing agency. All questions are multiple choice, and the test is completely automated — you'll get your results on the spot. The examinations for both brokers and salespersons are given in two parts. The first section on either examination is called the *Uniform Test* and consists of up to 100 general real estate questions. Most of those questions will determine your score, while roughly 10 to 15 questions, scattered throughout the exam, are being tested for future use. These "test questions" do not affect your score in any way. The second section, the *State Test*, consists of approximately 40 questions on Massachusetts law and practice — 30 questions on which your score will be based, plus 5 to 10 uncounted "test questions."

The content of the exam breaks down roughly as follows:

SALESPERSONS
Real Estate Law — 30%
Ownership and Transfer — 20%
Brokerage and Agency — 20%
Appraisal — 10%
Finance — 20%
Math Skills — 20%

BROKERS
Real Estate Law — 15%
Ownership and Transfer — 25%
Brokerage and Agency — 25%
Finance — 20%
Math Skills — 20%
Appraisal — 15%

The ASI approach to testing is designed to test your reasoning process as well as your real estate knowledge. The examination includes questions on general real estate information and the Massachusetts Real Estate License Law and Rules and Regulations, as well as math problems and several kinds of comprehension problems.

While the Massachusetts Real Estate License Examination is designed to find out how much you know, it also is designed to find out how well you can think and apply your knowledge in appropriate situations. Many of these questions involve reading comprehension: Can you read a statement or form and answer questions based on what you have read? Other questions involve reading comprehension in combination with application: Can you read a selection or problem and answer questions based on what you have read and what you know about certain real estate principles?

Throughout this *Supplement* you will find multiple-choice questions that follow the chapter sections. These questions are in the ASI test format. This format presents the question and four possible answers in a straightforward manner. There is only one correct answer to each question.

Math

Math problems relating to real estate transactions make up approximately 20 percent of the Massachusetts General Real Estate Examination. You may use a silent, hand-held, battery-operated calculator during the broker's and salesperson's license examinations.

The problems you will be asked to solve deal with the following subjects:

- Financing
- Tax Assessment
- Commissions
- Area Calculations
- Settlement Statement
- Profit and Loss
- Tax Ramifications

If you have difficulty with math, you should consider consulting *Mastering Real Estate Mathematics*, 6th Edition, by Ventolo, Tamper and Allaway, published by Real Estate Education Company, 155 North Wacker Drive, Chicago, IL 60606-1719. You will find an order form for this self-instructional text in the back of this supplement.

Test-Taking Strategies

- **Always read the question carefully**.

- If you know the correct answer, mark it and go on.

- If you are unsure of the correct answer, use the process of elimination to determine which answers are obviously wrong or have the least applicable relationship to the question. Eliminating just one answer increases your odds of a correct guess from 25 percent to 30 percent. Eliminate two incorrect answers, and your odds shoot up to fifty-fifty. Eliminate three incorrect answers, and you've hit the jackpot.

Intelligent guessing, however, will not ensure a passing score. Nor will knowing that a legal description problem may be included on the test help you pass if you cannot follow a metes-and-bounds description. Concentrate on learning the material by studying the main text and this *Supplement*, by working all the tests and exercises and, when you are done, by making sure that you can answer those questions you originally answered incorrectly.

Remember: Your most important preparation for the licensing examination involves studying and learning both general and Massachusetts-specific real estate principles and practices.

MASSACHUSETTS REAL ESTATE EXAMINATION CONTENT & STUDY GUIDE

UNIFORM TEST TOPIC	Modern Real Estate Practice, 14th ed. Chapter Number	Massachusetts Supplement, 5th ed. Chapter Number
Appraisals	18	18
Brokerage and Agency	4, 5, 6	4, 5
Contracts	11	10
Encumbrances and Liens	7, 10	9
Fair Housing Law	20	21
Finance	14, 15	14/15
Nature of Real Property	2, 3, 8	8
Property Management and Leases	16, 17	16
Public Control of Land	19	19/20
Tax Issues	3, 10	9, 11
Title and Transfer	7, 8, 12, 13, 22	6, 7
Voluntary and Involuntary Alienation	12	11

STATE TEST TOPIC	Massachusetts Supplement Chapter Number	Modern Real Estate Practice Chapter Number
Massachusetts Condominium and Time-Share Law	7	8
Massachusetts Fair Housing Law	21	20
Massachusetts State Licensing Law	13	—
Mandatory Disclosures	4, 21	4, 20
Massachusetts Real Estate Commission	13	—
State and Local Property Taxation	9	10
Statutory Regulation of Licensees	13	—
Zoning and Land Use Law	19/20	19

Real Estate Brokerage

NATURE OF THE BROKERAGE BUSINESS

Brokers and Salespersons

Massachusetts law distinguishes between two types of real estate professionals: real estate brokers and real estate salespersons.

A **real estate broker** is any person who sells, exchanges, purchases, rents or leases, or negotiates the sale, exchange, purchase, rental or leasing of any real estate or option on real estate, on someone else's behalf and for a fee or commission. Anyone who advertises or holds themselves out as engaged in activities related to the sale, exchange, purchase, leasing or renting of real estate falls under the broad statutory definition of "broker," as does anyone who procures prospects or assists or directs the negotiation or completion of any agreement or transaction that results or is intended to result in the sale, exchange, purchase, leasing or renting of any real estate.

The statutory definition of a **real estate salesperson** is identical to that of a broker, except that a salesperson does not engage in the completing of the negotiation of agreements or transactions aimed at exchanging, purchasing, renting or leasing real estate.

In Massachusetts, no salesperson may conduct or operate his or her own real estate business. All salespersons are required to affiliate with one broker, either as employees or independent contractors, and the broker must approve any transaction entered into by the salesperson. Salespersons are not entitled to commissions from anyone other than the broker who hold his or her license. Brokers are responsible for regulatory violations by their salespersons.

Because of the relationship between brokers and salespersons in Massachusetts, we will refer only to "brokers" throughout this chapter. Readers should understand, however, that the term "broker" as used in this chapter includes salespersons as well.

Compensation

A real estate broker works under a contractual agreement with his or her employer. In Massachusetts, this agreement may be created in one of three ways:

1. *Orally*

2. *In writing*

3. *By implication* — the broker and the seller *behave* as if they have an agreement.

A written agreement between the broker and the principal is not necessary to create an enforceable brokerage contract. The Statute of Frauds' requirement of a written agreement applies to conveyances of property, but does not apply to employment agreements such as listing contracts. However, brokers and salespersons are advised always to execute a written contract.

Students should clearly understand that two contracts are involved in a typical real estate transaction: the *listing agreement*, which is a service contract between the seller and the broker, and the *sales contract* between the seller and the buyer. Only the sales contract is required to be in writing, although an exclusive right to sell must also be written in order to be enforceable in court.

The essence of a listing contract between a seller and a broker is that the real estate professional will use his or her knowledge and skill to find a buyer who is ready, willing and able to purchase the property under the terms and conditions stated in the contract.

The broker must be careful to properly "list the property" (see Chapter 5), and to find out all the seller's terms and conditions. Such conditions include: (1) the asking price for the property; (2) any special financial considerations that may be involved; and (3) what personal property will be conveyed along with the house.

After a broker has done the job he or she was hired to do, he or she should be entitled to compensation. It sometimes bothers an owner when a broker rushes back to the office immediately after being hired, calls a prospective buyer whom he or she knows is looking for the type of property involved, and obtains a signed contract of sale with no apparent effort. Of course, the same owner is likely to squawk if the broker seems to be taking too long to find a buyer. However, the broker is paid for the *result*, whether it takes hours, days, weeks or months to produce a ready, willing and able buyer.

In the past, the general rule was that as soon as a broker produced a ready, willing and able buyer and a binding contract was signed, the commission was earned, whether or not the sale ever went to closing. Owners always have been able to protect themselves by including in the listing or the sales contract a provision that no commission is payable until the sale actually closes. A seller may also reserve the right, in the listing agreement, to reject any purchaser or to condition the commission on producing a buyer who meets certain specified requirements.

The Massachusetts Supreme Court has consistently held that a broker is entitled to

his or her commission only when the following three conditions are met:

1. The broker produces a purchaser ready, willing and able to buy on the terms fixed by the owner.

2. The purchaser enters into a binding contract with the owner to purchase the property.

3. The purchaser completes the transaction by closing the title in accordance with the provisions of the contract.

*A real estate broker under a brokerage agreement is entitled to a commission from the seller **only** if these three requirements are met.*

If the contract is not consummated because of the buyer's financial inability to perform, or because of any other buyer default, the broker has no right to a commission from the seller. However, a seller and a broker could agree in the written listing or sales contract on the extent to which the forfeited earnest money deposit might be shared in the event of a buyer's default. On the other hand, if the failure to complete the contract is the result of the seller's wrongful act or interference, the broker is entitled to receive a commission based on the contract presented. The listing contract might also include terms that a commission must be paid if the broker presents a customer who is ready, willing and able and the seller refuses to sign a contract.

Even if the broker succeeds in finding a ready, willing and able buyer who meets all the terms and conditions of sale described by the seller in the listing contract, however, he or she still has not earned a commission unless the seller signs a contract to sell. Should the owner refuse to sign a contract of sale, and as long as there is no bad faith in the refusal, no commission is earned (of course, the seller may be liable to the broker for damages). The practical reality of this rule is: get the seller's signature.

A broker can earn a commission, then, if the sale is not consummated because of the seller's default or the seller's decision not to complete the transaction. But remember: the seller must either enter into a contract to sell and then either refuse to comply or be dealing in bad faith.

Procuring Cause

In some cases, a broker may claim a commission by showing that he or she was the **procuring cause** of a sale even though the broker did not actually complete the terms of the employment agreement. Generally, the mere introduction of a potential buyer to a property does not entitle the broker a commission. The broker needs to demonstrate that he or she was the efficient, effective, or predominating means of bringing about the actual sale. Introducing a seller to a prospective buyer, or interesting a customer in a property that he or she later buys may satisfy that test. The broker's case is particularly strong if the seller impedes or precludes the broker from negotiations or involvement in the sale.

FOR EXAMPLE ...

Broker is hired with an open listing for an indefinite period of time and a 6 percent commission. On Monday, Broker shows Owner's house to Buyer. On Tuesday, Owner fires Broker. On Wednesday, Owner calls Buyer and negotiates the sale of the property.

Technically, Broker has not done her job — she did not present Owner with an offer from a ready, willing and able buyer. However, Broker was the *procuring cause* of the sale: she was responsible for Owner and Buyer getting together and for the property being sold. Broker could sue for a commission, and would be likely to win.

Normally, the courts examine the broker's continued efforts to consummate the sale as well as the good faith of both the buyer and the seller. A broker may often have a provision in the listing contract that says that he or she is entitled to a commission if the property is sold to a customer of the broker *within a specified period of time after the listing ends*. To protect all parties, owners should be provided with notices or lists of potential buyers to whom the property has been shown. The most difficult problem occurs when a buyer inquires about the property because of a sign that the broker has placed on it, and then buys the property directly from the owner.

Massachusetts courts will not generally allow a broker to collect a commission if the transaction that results is different from the original transaction. How it is different and why it is different are important considerations in determining the broker's entitlement to a commission. The court will consider whether or not some new force instigated the sale after the broker ended his or her efforts. The court examines each case on its own facts.

Multiple Commissions

Where one broker is the procuring cause, and another broker clinches the deal, the owner could end up having to pay more than one commission. While possibly burdensome for sellers, this ensures that everyone is compensated for doing their job. For instance, if the owner changes real estate agents after the expiration of a listing agreement, and the new agent sells the property to a buyer who originally contacted the first agent, the owner may owe commissions to both. The original broker's right to a commission is clear, because he or she introduced the buyer to the property and thus was the procuring cause. The second broker is entitled to a commission because he or she did exactly what was specified. There is no obligation to split a single commission. This is an excellent argument in favor of the exclusive listing contract, which will avoid this problem and is discussed in Chapter 5 in this *Supplement*.

Brokers or salespersons who are REALTORS® resolve these disputes by the rules of the association, so there are no multiple commission situations.

Attachment

When a broker is entitled to a commission and the seller refuses to pay, a writ of attachment may be filed against the seller's property. An *attachment* is a legal writ or proceeding by which property is made subject to a lien pending the outcome of a suit. By means of an attachment, the sale of the real estate is prohibited until the suit has been heard in court. If the owner attempts to close the sale, he or she will be obligated either to settle the suit by paying the commission, or somehow guarantee that the amount can be paid. The owner will not be able to transfer or sell the property until it is free of the attachment. Often, an owner cannot afford to wait for the suit to be heard and is forced to pay the commission.

When an attachment is sought, the courts may demand that notice be given the owner and that a hearing be held prior to the issuance of the writ of attachment. This process ensures that an owner will have an opportunity to demonstrate why the attachment is improper or to make other arrangements for guaranteeing the potential financial obligation.

The Law of Agency

The principal-agent relationship results from a contract of employment. In such a contract, the principal gives the agent authority to act on the principal's behalf, and the agent consents to that authority. Generally this "hiring" may be oral, although good practice involves the use of a signed listing contract. The rules and regulations of the Board of Registration of Real Estate Brokers and Salesmen require that hiring contracts for the exclusive right to sell *must* be in writing. (See Chapter 5 for an explanation of this type of listing.)

Because buyers of real estate often do not understand the law of agency, and typically believe that the person who drives them around town showing them properties is "their" agent, a disclosure requirement exists that requires each broker to have consumers sign an *agency disclosure* form at the first personal meeting. (See Figure 4.1.) This form makes clear to the consumer that the broker is working on behalf of the seller.

Massachusetts recognizes three forms of agency: seller's agent, buyer's agent, and disclosed dual agent. The three types of agency are listed and defined on the back of the required agency disclosure form.

Seller's Agent. A seller who engages the services of a listing broker is the broker's client, and the broker is the seller's agent. The broker/agent owes the seller/principal the traditional *fiduciary responsibilities* of care, obedience, accounting, loyalty and disclosure (the acronym "COALD") and must put the seller's lawful interests ahead of all others. The seller's agent must negotiate the best possible price and terms for the seller.

Buyer's Agent. A buyer who engages the services of a broker becomes the broker's client, and the broker is the buyer's agent. The broker/agent owes the buyer/principal the traditional fiduciary responsibilities of care, obedience, accounting, loyalty and disclosure (the acronym "COALD") and must negotiate the best price and terms for the buyer, whose lawful interests must be put ahead of all others. A buyer brokerage agreement appears in Figure 4.2.

Disclosed Dual Agent. A broker may represent both the buyer and the seller on the same property. To act as a dual agent, the broker must obtain the informed consent of both parties, and owes both buyer and seller a reduced fiduciary duty. However, while the dual agent is obliged to treat both parties with equal fairness and honesty, neither can expect the broker's undivided loyalty or total disclosure. An undisclosed dual agency is illegal, and a broker who acts on behalf of more than one party to a transaction without disclosure may lose his or her license. A dual agency disclosure form is reproduced in Figure 4.3.

CONSUMER PROTECTION LAW

In addition to the obligations placed on the broker by the fiduciary relationship, Massachusetts brokers must comply with the provisions of the Massachusetts Consumer Protection Act (MCPA) (Massachusetts General Law, Chapter 93A). The purpose of the MCPA is to level the playing field between consumers and businesses. The act outlaws unfair and deceptive acts or practices in the conduct of any trade or commerce, including advertising, offering for sale, rent or lease; or selling, renting, leasing or distributing any service or property whether real or personal, tangible or intangible.

The major significance of the act to the real estate broker is that it increases the broker's responsibility for his or her statements and omissions. Under common law, a broker could be held liable only for *intentional* misstatements he or she made to the buyer. If the broker received inaccurate information from the seller and passed it on in good faith to the buyer, the broker generally could not be found guilty of misrepresentation. But under the MCPA, the broker can be held liable for *any* untrue claim or representation made to the buyer, whether directly, indirectly or by implication, as well as for omissions and nonstatements. *Fraudulent intent need not be proven for such a claim to be considered illegal.* In practice this means that if a seller gives a broker false information and the broker then presents this information as fact, the broker can be held liable for misrepresentation.

Because the act is designed to provide equal bargaining power, facts that a broker *should* know need to be disclosed if they would tend to caution a buyer against entering into a contract. The fact that the buyer never asked a question about something important relating to the property does not relieve the broker of the responsibility to disclose relevant information.

In addition to this broad statement of liability, the act lists specific actions considered to be misrepresentations. These include:

- making false claims about a product's construction, durability, safety or strength;

- making false claims concerning the ease with which a product can be repaired or maintained;

- making false claims about financing terms or availability;

- advertising that something has a quality, value or usability that it does not have;

- substituting different goods for those advertised ("bait and switch"); and

- offering guarantees without disclosing the nature and extent of the guarantees.

The act makes no exception for "puffing" in advertising or otherwise. Puffing is an exaggerated or superlative comment or opinion not made as a representation of fact. Under common law, puffing was permitted; fraudulent misrepresentation of fact was not. But the MCPA makes no distinction between claims presented as fact and those presented as opinion.

The broker may be held liable for a misstatement in an advertisement even if he or she later informs the prospective buyer that the statement was incorrect.

All representations that have the capacity to deceive buyers or influence them in any way have been declared illegal, including those that were previously considered to be mere sales rhetoric.

Affirmative Disclosure

Equally important under the MCPA is the broker's duty to disclose all facts relating to the sale. In the past, sellers and brokers were required under common law only to disclose defects they knew about that could not be discovered in a normal inspection of the premises. Now, however, it is illegal to fail to disclose to a buyer or prospective buyer any fact that might influence the buyer or prospective buyer not to enter into the transaction, *whether or not the buyer or prospective buyer requests the information*.

Whether the buyer actually would have refused to complete the transaction if certain facts were disclosed appears to be immaterial — the possibility alone of such a refusal seems to constitute a violation of the law on the broker's part. A broker may also be held responsible even if the buyer agrees to purchase the property under conditions other than those originally agreed on (such as a lower price).

Persons Affected by the Law

The MCPA applies to all listing, selling and cooperating brokers and all salespersons affiliated with these brokers as either employees or independent contractors. Sellers, developers and builders also come under the Act's authority. However, *the law does not apply to owners who sell their homes privately*. The Massachusetts Supreme Court has reasoned that because buyers and private sellers enjoy equal rights under the common law, extending the Act's protection to buyers involved in private sales would give them an unnecessary advantage.

The broker is also a vendor of services, and the degree to which he or she advertises or makes claims about the speed, quality or diligence of these services brings the broker-owner (and broker-seller) relationship under the MCPA. The substantial impact on the landlord-tenant relationship under this act is discussed in Chapter 16.

Enforcement

The attorney general of Massachusetts has the power to issue rules and regulations for interpreting and enforcing the act. Although the attorney general may intervene whenever a violation occurs, usually this only happens when a violation involves a large number of consumers. Individuals who have sustained

losses as a result of unfair or deceptive practices may bring suit themselves. A consumer must first give the alleged violator 30 days' written notice of the claim, describing the unfair practice and the resulting loss so that the accused can investigate the claim and offer to settle it out of court. *If the consumer rejects the offer and a court finds that it was indeed reasonable, the consumer may recover no more than the amount of the offer*.

If the court does not consider the offer reasonable, the consumer may be awarded the amount of actual damages or $25, whichever is greater. The court may double or triple the amount of damages if (1) the unfair or deceptive act or practice was a willful and knowing violation, or (2) the accused refuses in bad faith to make a reasonable offer to settle. Multiple damages will not be awarded if the accused did not violate the act willfully, although the consumer will still receive attorney's fees.

Recommendations

If the broker knows of a problem or discovers one during an inspection, he or she must disclose that information to the buyer or prospective buyer, identify its source and state whether or not he or she has verified it. When the broker makes any sort of claim or representation, he or she should disclose both the source and whether or not he or she has made an attempt to personally verify that information. *The broker cannot be held responsible for the truthfulness of the claims if he or she has not tried to verify them*. However, if the broker has tried to verify the claims or received information that could be used for verification, he or she must say so. The broker is not required to conduct any investigation of property that is beyond his or her level of competence.

Cooperating brokers also must identify the source of their representations and disclose their attempts at verification and any facts that might cause the prospective buyer not to complete the transaction. Cooperating brokers should make independent investigations of property they are involved with whenever possible.

The MCPA overrides the common-law agency duty of confidentiality in some circumstances. A broker must disclose *facts about the property* to the buyer even if the seller revealed them to the broker in confidence. If the seller has stated that the roof leaks, for example, the broker must pass on this information to the prospective buyer. But the broker need not reveal any personal information about the seller, such as the seller's willingness to accept an offer that is less than the listing price.

For a buyer to recover damages for the nondisclosure of a material fact, the buyer must prove that: (1) the seller or broker knew of the material defect; (2) the seller or broker failed to disclose the problem; and (3) if the buyer had known of the defect, he or she would not have purchased the property.

To help the broker prove that he or she did not mislead the buyer, a special clause has been added to the revised standard purchase and sale agreement issued by the Greater Boston Real Estate Board. The clause requires buyers to list the representations the broker has made that they relied on when deciding to make the purchase.

FOR EXAMPLE ...

I

Seller knows that 20 acres of his 100-acre property have been used as a dumping ground for hazardous and toxic materials since 1974. When he sells to Buyer, who plans to build a health spa and retreat center on the land, both Seller and his broker "forget" to mention the contamination. Seller will be liable to Buyer.

II

Broker showed Purchasers a house in their price range. They were new to the city, and asked about the safety of the neighborhood. Broker replied that it was "okay." Three days after they moved in, the Purchasers' new home was burglarized, and they sued Broker for misrepresentation. Broker is not liable if he had no knowledge of any facts suggesting that the neighborhood was unsafe.

TERMINATION

The agency relationship may be terminated at will by either the principal or the agent. Neither party has to have a reason to terminate the agency, and the broker cannot claim expenses from the principal unless this was specifically provided for in the hiring contract. If, however, the agency contract provides that the relationship is to continue for a specific period of time, such as an exclusive right to sell for 90 days, early termination exposes the seller to a potential lawsuit for expenses and damages by the broker. If the broker has done something wrong that gives the seller "good cause" to terminate the contract, or if the seller removes the property from the market, then the likelihood that the broker will recover compensation for expenses incurred or a commission if the property is sold is considerably lessened.

THE MASSACHUSETTS REAL ESTATE LICENSE LAW

The Massachusetts Real Estate License Law and the rules and regulations of the Board of Registration of Real Estate Brokers and Salesmen will be the subject matter of questions on your state license examination and the law that governs your professional life after you are licensed (see Chapter 13).

Figure 4.1   Agency Disclosure

MASSACHUSETTS BOARD OF REGISTRATION OF REAL ESTATE BROKERS AND SALESPERSONS
MANDATORY AGENCY DISCLOSURE - AGENCY RELATIONSHIP

The purpose of this disclosure is to enable you to make informed choices before working with a real estate licensee. It must be provided at the first personal meeting that you have with an agent to discuss a specific property. THIS IS NOT A CONTRACT. It is a disclosure notice for your information and protection. BE SURE TO READ THE DESCRIPTIONS OF THE DIFFERENT TYPES OF AGENCY REPRESENTATION ON THE OTHER SIDE OF THIS DISCLOSURE.

CONSUMER INFORMATION

1. Whether you are the buyer or the seller you can choose to have the advice, assistance and representation of your own agent. Do not assume that a broker is acting on your behalf unless you have contracted with that broker to represent you.

2. All real estate licensees must, by law, present properties honestly and accurately.

3. If you are a seller you may authorize your listing agent to cooperate with agents from other firms to help sell your property. These cooperating agents may be subagents who work for the seller or buyer's agents.

4. If you are the buyer you have the option of working with sellers' or buyers' agents. This decision will depend on the types of services you want from a real estate agent. A buyer should tell sellers' agents, including subagents, only what he/she would tell the seller directly.

CONSUMER RESPONSIBILITY

The duties of a real estate licensee do not relieve the consumer of the responsibility to protect his/her own interest. Consumers with questions on whether and how real estate agents share fees should pose them to the agent. If you need advice for legal, tax, insurance or other matters it is your responsibility to consult a professional in those areas.

ACKNOWLEDGEMENT

I have provided this disclosure form to _____.
(print name/s of consumer/s)

I have informed the above named consumer/s that I am a: (check one)   ☐ Seller's Agent
   ☐ Buyer's Agent

_____   _____   _____   _____, 19 _____
(Signature of Real Estate Agent)   (License No.)   (Month)   (Day)   (Year)

I have read this agency disclosure form IN ITS ENTIRETY ON BOTH SIDES. I understand that this form is for agency disclosure AND NOT A CONTRACT. It was provided to me by the agent named above.

_____   _____   _____, 19 _____   (check one)   ☐ Buyer
(Signature/s of Consumer/s)   (Month)   (Day)   (Year)   ☐ Seller

☐ As a consumer I decline to sign this disclosure.

Figure 4.2   Buyer Brokerage Agreement

BUYER BROKERAGE AGREEMENT

THIS AGREEMENT is made by and between _____ (the "Buyer") and
_____ (the "Broker")

In consideration of the following mutual agreements, the undersigned hereby agree as follows:

1. The Buyer grants to the Broker the sole and exclusive right to arrange for the acquisition by the Buyer of property of the type generally described as follows (the "Property"):

2. The term of this agreement shall commence on _____, 199__ and terminate on _____, 199__.

3. The Broker shall use reasonably diligent efforts to locate the Property and to negotiate terms and conditions of a contract acceptable to the Buyer (the "Contract") providing for the acquisition of the Property by the Buyer. The Contract may consist of an accepted offer, purchase and sale agreement, option, deed, exchange agreement or any other instrument under which such acquisition may take place.

4. The Buyer shall pay to the Broker a retainer in the amount of $ _____ as compensation for professional counselling, consultation and research. Such retainer is payable upon execution of this agreement and is non-refundable, but shall [ ] / shall not [ ] be credited against any fee payable under the following paragraph.

5. The Broker will be deemed to have earned a full fee hereunder (a) in the event that, during the term of this agreement, the Buyer or any other person acting for the Buyer or on the Buyer's behalf (the "Buyer's Nominee") enters into the Contract or otherwise acquires the Property, whether through the services of the Broker or otherwise, or (b) in the event that, within _____ months following the term of this agreement, the Buyer or the Buyer's Nominee enters into the Contract or otherwise acquires the Property after receiving information about the Property from the Broker during said term. The fee shall be equal to:
_____
This fee shall be payable at such time as the Buyer or the Buyer's Nominee (a) takes title to the Property, (b) assigns the Contract or (c) if the Contract consists of an option, allows such option to lapse without exercise thereof.

6. The Broker may cooperate with, and pay compensation to, other brokers and their agents in connection with the performance of the Broker's services hereunder. In addition, the Broker may simultaneously service the needs of more than one buyer interested in acquiring the same type of property.

7. Any compensation received by the Broker either directly from a seller or in the form of a fee offered by a listing broker shall be disclosed to the Buyer and shall be credited against the amounts payable hereunder by the Buyer, who shall remain liable for any deficiency.

8. The Buyer shall cooperate fully with the Broker's efforts to arrange for the acquisition of the Property.

EXECUTED under seal as of the _____ day of _____, 199 ___.

_____
(Buyer)

_____
(Broker)
By_____

Its_____
       title (duly-authorized)

UNDER THE CODE OF ETHICS AND STANDARDS OF PRACTICE OF THE NATIONAL ASSOCIATION OF REALTORS®, ANY REALTOR® ENTERING INTO A CONTRACT TO REPRESENT A BUYER MUST ADVISE THE POTENTIAL CLIENT OF:

1. THE REALTOR'S® GENERAL COMPANY POLICIES REGARDING COOPERATION WITH OTHER FIRMS, AND
2. ANY POTENTIAL FOR THE REALTOR® TO ACT AS A DISCLOSED DUAL AGENT ON BEHALF OF THE SELLER AS WELL AS THE BUYER.

Source: This form has been made available through the courtesy of the Greater Boston Real Estate Board, and is protected by the copyright laws.

Figure 4.3   Dual Agency Disclosure and Agreement Form

THIS IS A LEGALLY BINDING CONTRACT. IF NOT UNDERSTOOD, SEEK LEGAL ADVICE.
DUAL AGENCY DISCLOSURE AND AGREEMENT

The undersigned Seller and Buyer acknowledge that _____ ("Broker"), through its Agent(s) _____, is undertaking a **"disclosed dual agency"** representation for the sale of the property located at _____.

Under the provisions of the Agency Disclosure Regulation, effective July 2, 1993, "disclosed dual agency" representation is permitted in Massachusetts. "Disclosed dual agency" is defined as follows:

DISCLOSED DUAL AGENT

"A broker can work for both the buyer and seller on the same property provided such broker obtains the informed consent of both parties. The broker is then considered a disclosed dual agent. This broker owes the seller and the buyer a duty to deal with them fairly and honestly. In this type of agency relationship the broker does not represent either the seller or buyer exclusively and they cannot expect the broker's undivided loyalty. Also, undisclosed dual agency is illegal."

The Buyer and the Seller acknowledge that they have been fully informed about both the advantages and limitations of this type of representation. The Buyer and the Seller should read the following information and understand it before signing below.

The Buyer and the Seller recognize and acknowledge that this document does not replace any documents signed earlier, such as the buyer agency agreement signed by the Buyer on _____ and the listing agreement signed by the Seller on _____. However, where this document contradicts or conflicts with any earlier signed documents, this Dual Agency Disclosure And Agreement shall replace and supersede all earlier documents.

In the event that the Buyer and the Seller do not enter into an agreement for the sale or lease of real estate, or in the event that the time set for closing the transaction expires, the Broker may terminate this dual agency by mailing or delivering written notice to the Buyer and the Seller.

What the Broker and its Agents can do and will do for the Seller and the Buyer when acting as a Disclosed Dual Agent:

1. We will provide accurate information to the Buyer and the Seller.
2. We must disclose to the Buyer all material facts about the property that are known to us.
3. We will disclose to the Seller information concerning the financial qualifications of the Buyer.
4. We will explain real estate principles to the Buyer and the Seller.
5. We can assist the Buyer in obtaining property inspections.
6. We can explain closing costs and procedures to the Buyer and the Seller.
7. We can assist the Buyer in comparing financial alternatives.
8. We can assist the Buyer in the Buyer's attempt to obtain a mortgage loan commitment.
9. We can provide information on comparable sales so that the Buyer and the Seller can assess the property's market value.
10. We will assist with the completion of all appropriate sales contracts, including the necessary protection and disclosure for both the Buyer and the Seller.
11. We will disclose to both the Buyer and the Seller our fees and how they are to be paid.

What the Broker and its Agents cannot disclose to the Buyer and the Seller:

1. We cannot disclose confidential information that we may know about either party without that party's written permission.
2. We cannot disclose any price that the Seller may take other than the listing price without the written permission of the Seller.
3. We cannot disclose any price that the Buyer may be willing to pay other than the offer price without the written permission of the Buyer.
4. We cannot recommend or suggest an offer price to the Buyer or a counteroffer price to the Seller.

CAUTION: The parties must understand that any agreement between the seller and the Buyer regarding the final sale price and terms is the result of negotiations between the Seller and the Buyer acting in their own best interest and on their own behalf.

The parties agree to attach a copy of this signed Dual Agency Disclosure And Agreement to the Purchase and Sales Agreement.

By signing below, you are giving the Broker your informed permission to act as Disclosed Dual Agent in this transaction. Please do not sign until you feel sufficiently informed to be completely comfortable with this arrangement.

[SIGNATURES]

All parties agree to sign below at the time of entering into the Purchase and Sales Agreement to reaffirm and acknowledge their intent to enter into the above Dual Agency Disclosure and Agreement.

[SIGNATURES]

Questions

1. An enforceable listing agreement does not have to be in writing because:

   a. the broker has a fiduciary relationship with the principal.
   b. the principal has a fiduciary relationship with the broker.
   c. the law of agency does not apply in the case of a listing agreement.
   d. the Statute of Frauds does not apply to a listing agreement.

2. Which of the following is *not* a necessary for a broker to be entitled to a commission?

   a. A signed listing agreement
   b. A ready, willing and able buyer
   c. Closing of title by purchaser
   d. A binding contract between seller and purchaser

3. The Consumer Protection Law requires that:

   a. the broker keep all information that the seller has provided confidential.
   b. the broker disclose everything that the seller tells him or her.
   c. the broker disclose information that might affect the sale even though the buyer does not ask for it.
   d. the seller disclose all facts that might affect the sale.

4. Six months after the buyer bought a house the roof leaked during a rainstorm. When the house was listed, the seller told the broker that the roof leaked, but they agreed not to tell any prospective buyers. The broker claims that the buyer did not ask about the roof. Under these facts the buyer:

   a. can sue the broker under MCPA.
   b. cannot sue the broker under MCPA.
   c. can sue the seller under MCPA.
   d. cannot do anything because the leaking roof could have been discovered by inspection.

5. A buyer's agent:

   a. owes the buyer the traditional fiduciary duties.
   b. retains the right to hire subagents.
   c. must obtain the informed consent of all parties.
   d. may act on behalf of both buyer and seller.

6. Care, obedience, accounting, loyalty and disclosure are the:

   a. responsibilities required by the MCPA.
   b. elements required to prove that an agent is entitled to a commission.
   c. traditional fiduciary duties owed by a principal to an agent.
   d. traditional fiduciary duties owed by the agent to the principal.

7. A broker is legally entitled to a commission if he or she:

   a. produces a buyer who is (1) ready, (2) willing and (3) able.
   b. (1) produces a purchaser and (2) a binding contract, and (3) the transaction closes.
   c. has a signed listing contract.
   d. introduces the seller to the eventual purchaser.

8. Broker A shows Owner's house to Buyer on March 7. On March 10, A's listing expires, and Owner lists the house with Broker B. On March 15, Buyer calls B and asks to see the house again. On May 1, the sale closes. With regard to the commission:

   a. A is entitled to nothing.
   b. A and B are both entitled to a full commission.
   c. A is entitled to ½ of B's commission.
   d. A is entitled to all of B's commission.

9. An agency relationship may be terminated:

   a. only for "good cause."
   b. only under the terms of the contract.
   c. at will by either party.
   d. only if one party breaches the contract.

10. What are the three types of agency recognized in Massachusetts?

    a. Seller's, buyer's, undisclosed dual.
    b. Subagency, disclosed dual, seller's.
    c. Seller's, buyer's, disclosed dual.
    d. Seller's, buyer's, full fiduciary.

5

Listing Agreements

LISTING PROPERTY

The *listing agreement* is the employment contract between the real estate broker and the seller. It contains the essential substance of the transaction: it defines the relationship between the agent and principal and establishes their rights and responsibilities; it sets the price of the property and the rate of commission that will be paid to the broker. The listing agreement may establish such things as whether or not the seller will permit the broker to cooperate with buyers' brokers, whether or not a multiple listing service may be used, and whether or not a lock box may be placed on the property. In short, the listing agreement sets out the parties' responsibilities and expectations.

The types of listing agreements commonly used in Massachusetts include the exclusive-right-to-sell listing, the exclusive agency listing, the open listing and the co-broker listing.

Listing Agreements

Exclusive-Right-to-Sell Listing. In an exclusive-right-to-sell listing, the broker has sole control over the sale of the property. This type of listing is the most desirable for brokers because, in addition to total control over the transaction, it provides them with the greatest protection. By law, the contract must be *in writing* and signed by the parties involved. A definite period of time must be stated, at the end of which the exclusive right to sell will terminate. As with all written documents that a broker asks anyone to sign, the broker must furnish the parties with a copy. Two examples of exclusive-right-to-sell agreements are found in Figures 5.1 and 5.2.

Exclusive Agency Listing. An exclusive agency listing is similar to the exclusive-right-to-sell, in that it strictly limits the parties by whom the property may be sold. In this listing arrangement, however, the owner reserves the right to sell the property without the broker's assistance, in which case the owner keeps the commission. The broker, on the other hand, is hired as the only broker who will represent the owner in the sale and is entitled to the commission if he or she produces a ready, willing and able buyer. The contract should be in writing and for a specific term. An exclusive agency agreement is illustrated in Figure 5.3.

Open Listing. Under an open listing, the owner retains the right to hire as many brokers as he or she pleases. The first broker to present a ready, willing and able buyer earns the commission, and the other brokers are automatically discharged. An open listing hiring contract may be oral or written. An open listing agreement commonly used in Massachusetts is shown in Figure 5.4.

Co-Broker Agreement. It is not unusual for one broker to have a property listed that meets the needs of a buyer found by another broker. The co-broker agreement between the listing broker and the cooperating or "finding" broker permits the listing broker to show the property to the finding broker's customer. If the customer buys the property, the listing broker will divide the commission between the two brokers in whatever proportion is agreed to in the contract. The listing broker retains control of the listing, and the cooperating broker acts in the capacity of a salesperson bringing a customer to the listing broker. It is the listing broker, however, who must complete the transaction. The co-broker agreement should be expressed in writing even if the two brokers have had previous dealings.

Net Listing. Under the Massachusetts Real Estate License Law, a "net" listing isforbidden. A net listing results when an owner specifies a particular dollar amount that he or she must "net" from the sale of the property; any sum exceeding that amount will constitute the broker's commission. In those states in which such arrangements are legal, they often result in disagreements between owners and brokers on methods of payment, and in claims that brokers have set prices and made exorbitant profits. Under a net listing it is difficult to balance the broker's fiduciary responsibility to the principal with the brokers' own ability to make a profit. Because the practice of net listing is illegal in Massachusetts, brokers must inform owners that their fee will be a percentage of the selling price, or a flat fee for services. Then the broker presents the buyer with information about comparable sales in the area, and the seller then determines the proper sales price, based on the broker's advice and expertise.

FOR EXAMPLE ...

Ben Bottomline called Doris Doright, a Boston real estate broker, and told her that he wanted to sell his house.

"I don't want to be bothered with percentages and bargaining and offers and counter-offers," he explained. "I just need to walk out of this deal with $150,000 in my pocket. You sell this place for any more than that, and you keep the rest."

Doright knew that homes such as Bottomline's in his neighborhood were selling for over $200,000. On the other hand, she knew that a net listing is illegal in Massachusetts. What should she do?

PRICING THE PROPERTY

Brokers are often asked for their opinion of a property's market value before it is listed for sale. Sellers rightly assume that a broker should be generally knowledgeable about local property values. In order to protect the

seller's interests, and to ensure that a fair and reasonable price is set, a broker should prepare a *competitive market analysis* (CMA) that compares the seller's property with similar properties that have sold recently. The broker may advise the seller of how the price the seller has set compares with other known values, and encourage the seller to consider such factors as how quickly he or she wants to sell. However, a licensed broker should avoid recommending or setting a price on the listed property. *It is the seller's responsibility to set the selling price.*

A comparative market analysis is not an appraisal and must not be presented as one. In Massachusetts, no one other than a state-certified residential real estate appraiser or state-licensed real estate appraiser may appraise real estate (see Chapter 18). Real estate brokers or salespersons, however, are permitted to give price opinions in the normal course of their business *as long as the opinion is not referred to as an appraisal.* Non-appraisers may appraise property in non-federally related transactions, such as those not involving federal mortgage insurance or guarantees. While a listing agreement or a strictly cash sale is not a federally-related transactions, most mortgage applications are likely to be, and so would require the involvement of a certified or licensed appraiser (see Chapter 18).

Whether or not they are licensed appraisers, brokers should disclose to sellers whatever information they have about a property's value. If necessary, they should express concern about a seller's price, although they may not give an opinion as to what the proper selling price should be.

While counseling sellers about a property's price, brokers should emphasize that any information they present is neither an opinion of value nor an appraisal, but merely important information that they feel should be shared with the seller. If further questions arise, or if the seller is insistent, the broker should recommend that a licensed appraiser be consulted.

Figure 5.1 Exclusive-Right-to-Sell Listing Agreement

EXCLUSIVE RIGHT TO SELL LISTING AGREEMENT

_____, 19_____

To: _____

In consideration of your submitting the listing information with respect to my real property (the "property") which is attached hereto, to the Multiple Listing Service within three (3) days and of your efforts to find a buyer for the property, I hereby give you from _____, 19 _____ to _____, 19 _____ inclusive, the same being the term of the listing, the sole right to sell or exchange the property

at _____

for _____ Dollars $ _____.

I also agree that if you procure a buyer for the property, or if said property is sold or exchanged by you, by me, or by anyone else, during the continuance of this contract, or if within _____ thereafter the property shall be sold or exchanged to or with any person to whom the property has been shown prior to the expiration of the term of this contract either for the price above set forth or for any other price or upon any other terms which may be acceptable to me, I will pay you a fee of _____ for professional services, the same as I would if you had made the sale or exchange yourself. However, I shall not be obligated to pay such fee if a valid listing is entered into during the term of said protection period with another licensed real estate broker.

The property is offered without respect to race, color, religion, national origin, gender, sexual orientation, age, marital status, veteran status, presence of children, receipt of public assistance or mental or physical handicaps. You may make arrangements with any other real estate broker to act as a sub-agent in connection with the sale or exchange of the property on the condition that any sub-agent's compensation will be payable from your commission. In the event that you desire to show the property in cooperation with a licensed real estate agent who is representing a prospective buyer, I authorize you to compensate the agent of any prospective buyer an amount to be determined by you.

I have disclosed the information set forth herein with regard to the property, including all improvements, equipment and fixtures therein, to you. I hereby authorize you to disclose said information and any other information which you may obtain or discover regarding the property to a buyer, prospective buyer, or licensed real estate agent who is representing a prospective buyer, or your agents or subagents. I further authorize you to include, print or publish the same upon any Multiple Listing Service Form, Offer to Purchase Form and/or Purchase and Sale Agreement Form or any other writing or document as you may use.

I agree to supply smoke detector certification.

All deposits shall be held by you as my agent and shall be duly accounted for at the time for performance of an agreement. You shall be entitled to receive from me an amount equal to _____ of any deposit forfeited by any buyer and retained by me as long as the amount shall not be more than the fee referred to above. I agree that in the event a dangerous level of lead is found in the property, I will report same as required by applicable law. I also agree that once I have entered into a Purchase and Sale Agreement with a buyer and during the pendency of said agreement, you shall have no obligation to present further offers to me or to continue marketing the property.

I hereby authorize the photographing of the property and the use of such photographs in promoting its sale or exchange. I also agree that you may show the property at any reasonable hour. I agree that the responsibility for the care of the property shall not be yours and you shall not be liable to me for any damages which may occur to the property.

I have checked this Listing Agreement and agree that, together with any changes assented to by me, it is complete and accurate to the best of my knowledge. I acknowledge that the information contained in the accompanying data sheet was supplied by me and not checked for accuracy by you. I agree to indemnify and hold you harmless from any and all claims, demands, causes of action, suits, damages, costs or expenses, including reasonable attorney's fees incurred by you on account of any misrepresentation or error made by me in providing you with the listing information, specifically including without limitation, any misrepresentation or error regarding the presence or absence of urea formaldehyde foam insulation. I further agree that in the event I default under this Agreement, you shall be entitled to collect from me, in addition to the fee set forth above, all costs and expenses, including attorney's fees, incurred by you on account of such default. If more than one person signs this Listing Agreement, the obligations contained herein shall be joint and several and bind all signatories.

Permission is granted to place a For Sale sign upon the property.	☐ Yes	☐ No
Permission is granted to place a lockbox on the property.	☐ Yes	☐ No
I have received a copy of the Agency Disclosure Form.	☐ Yes	☐ No
Does the property contain UFFI?	☐ Yes	☐ No
Is there an inground fuel tank on the property?	☐ Yes	☐ No

Witness my/our hand(s) and seal(s)

DATE _____   _____ OWNER

DATE _____   _____ OWNER

BROKER _____

DATE _____   BY _____

COPYRIGHT© 1994 GREATER SPRINGFIELD ASSOCIATION OF REALTORS®, INC.   LISTAGRE.PM4 Rev 7/94

Source: This form has been made available through the courtesy of the Greater Springfield Association of REALTORS®, and is protected by the copyright laws.

Figure 5.2   Agreement for Exclusive Right to Sell

AGREEMENT FOR EXCLUSIVE RIGHT TO SELL

DATE: _____

THIS AGREEMENT concerns the following property:_____
_____
_____   PRICE $ _____

In consideration of the mutual covenants and agreements herein contained, the undersigned Seller hereby gives to the undersigned Broker the sole and exclusive right to sell the said property for the price and on the terms and conditions herein set forth.

I. The Broker agrees:
   a. To use reasonable efforts to procure a ready, willing, and able Buyer of the property in accordance with the price, terms, and conditions of this Agreement.

II. The Broker is granted the sole authority to: *(Check if applicable)*
   [ ] a. Advertise the property;
   [ ] b. Post "For Sale" signs on the property;
   [ ] c. Cooperate with subagents; and/or
   [ ] d. Offer compensation to buyer agents.
      (NOTE: Regardless of how compensated, buyer agents represent the interests of buyers, not sellers.)

III. The Seller agrees:
   a. To refer all inquiries and offers for the purchase of said property to the Broker;
   b. To cooperate with the Broker in every reasonable way;
   c. To pay the Broker a fee for professional services of _____ if:
      (1) A Buyer is procured ready, willing, and able to buy said property, or any part thereof, in accordance with the price, terms and conditions of this Agreement, or such other price, terms and conditions as shall be acceptable to the Seller, whether or not the transaction proceeds; or
      (2) The said property, or any part thereof, is sold through the efforts of anyone including the Seller; or
      (3) The said property, or any part thereof, is sold within _____ days after the term of this Agreement to anyone who was introduced to the said property through the efforts of the Broker or his agents prior to the expiration of said term. However, no fee will be payable under this clause if the said property is sold after said term with the participation of a licensed broker to whom the Seller is obligated to pay a fee under the terms of a subsequent written exclusive listing agreement.

Once an offer has been accepted in writing and a transaction is pending, the Broker shall have no obligation to present further offers to the Seller.

IV. The Seller understands and agrees that the property will be marketed in compliance with all applicable fair housing laws.

V. The period of this Agreement shall be from _____, 199 ___, to and including
_____, 199 ___. Time is of the essence hereof.

Additional terms and conditions: _____
_____
_____

IN WITNESS WHEREOF, the Seller and the Broker have hereunto set their hands and seals as of the _____ day of
_____, 199 ____.

BROKER _____   SELLER _____

By_____

Its_____   SELLER _____
    title (duly-authorized)

UNDER THE CODE OF ETHICS AND STANDARDS OF PRACTICE OF THE NATIONAL ASSOCIATION OF REALTORS®, ANY REALTOR® ENTERING INTO A LISTING CONTRACT MUST ADVISE THE SELLER OF

1. THE REALTOR'S® GENERAL COMPANY POLICIES REGARDING COOPERATION WITH SUBAGENTS, THE PAYMENT OF COMPENSATION TO BUYER AGENTS, OR BOTH;
2. THE FACT THAT BUYER AGENTS, EVEN IF COMPENSATED BY THE LISTING BROKER OR BY THE SELLER, WILL REPRESENT THE INTERESTS OF BUYERS; AND
3. ANY POTENTIAL FOR THE LISTING BROKER TO ACT AS A DISCLOSED DUAL AGENT ON BEHALF OF THE SELLER AS WELL AS THE BUYER.

COPYRIGHT © 1984,1987,1993
GREATER BOSTON REAL ESTATE BOARD

All rights reserved. This form may not be copied or reproduced in whole or in part in any manner whatsoever without the prior express written consent of the Greater Boston Real Estate Board.

Source: This form has been made available through the courtesy of the Greater Boston Real Estate Board, and is protected by the copyright laws.

Figure 5.3   Agreement for Exclusive Agency

THIS AGREEMENT concerns the following property:_____
_____ PRICE $ _____

In consideration of the mutual covenants and agreements herein contained, the undersigned Seller hereby gives to the undersigned Broker the sole and exclusive agency to sell the said property for the price and on the terms and conditions herein set forth.

I. The Broker agrees:
   a. To use reasonable efforts to procure a ready, willing, and able Buyer of the property in accordance with the price, terms, and conditions of this Agreement.

II. The Broker is granted the sole authority to: *(Check if applicable)*
   [ ] a. Advertise the property;
   [ ] b. Post "For Sale" signs on the property;
   [ ] c. Cooperate with subagents; and/or
   [ ] d. Offer compensation to buyer agents.
       (NOTE: Regardless of how compensated, buyer agents represent the interests of buyers, not sellers.)

III. The Seller agrees:
   a. To refer all inquiries and offers made by or through any real estate agent for the purchase of said property to the Broker;
   b. To cooperate with the Broker in every reasonable way;
   c. To pay the Broker a fee for professional services of _____ if:
      (1) The Broker procures a Buyer ready, willing, and able to buy said property, or any part thereof, in accordance with the price, terms and conditions of this Agreement, or such other price, terms and conditions as shall be acceptable to the Seller, whether or not the transaction proceeds; or
      (2) The said property, or any part thereof, is sold through the efforts or with the assistance or participation (directly or indirectly) of the Broker or any other real estate agent; or
      (3) The said property, or any part thereof, is sold within _____ months after the term of this Agreement to anyone who was introduced to the said property through the efforts of the Broker or his agents prior to the expiration of said term. However, no fee will be payable under this clause if the said property is sold after said term with the participation of a licensed broker to whom the Seller is obligated to pay a fee under the terms of a subsequent written exclusive listing agreement.
      It is specifically understood and agreed that no fee will be payable by the Seller under this Agreement in any case where no real estate agent has directly or indirectly furnished information about the said property to the Buyer or otherwise assisted or participated in the sale in any way.

   Once an offer has been accepted in writing and a transaction is pending, the Broker shall have no obligation to present further offers to the Seller.

IV. The Seller understands and agrees that the property will be marketed in compliance with all applicable fair housing laws.

V. The period of this Agreement shall be from _____, 199 ___, to and including
_____, 199 ___. Time is of the essence hereof.

Additional terms and conditions: _____
_____
_____

   IN WITNESS WHEREOF, the Seller and the Broker have hereunto set their hands and seals as of the _____ day of
_____, 199 ____.

_____   _____
BROKER   SELLER

By_____   _____
            SELLER

Its_____
   title (duly-authorized)

UNDER THE CODE OF ETHICS AND STANDARDS OF PRACTICE OF THE NATIONAL ASSOCIATION OF REALTORS®, ANY REALTOR® ENTERING INTO A LISTING CONTRACT MUST ADVISE THE SELLER OF

1. THE REALTOR'S® GENERAL COMPANY POLICIES REGARDING COOPERATION WITH SUBAGENTS, THE PAYMENT OF COMPENSATION TO BUYER AGENTS, OR BOTH;
2. THE FACT THAT BUYER AGENTS, EVEN IF COMPENSATED BY THE LISTING BROKER OR BY THE SELLER, WILL REPRESENT THE INTERESTS OF BUYERS; AND
3. ANY POTENTIAL FOR THE LISTING BROKER TO ACT AS A DISCLOSED DUAL AGENT ON BEHALF OF THE SELLER AS WELL AS THE BUYER.

Source: This form has been made available through the courtesy of the Greater Boston Real Estate Board, and is protected by the copyright laws.

Figure 5.4   Open Listing Agreement

OPEN LISTING AGREEMENT

DATE: _____

THIS AGREEMENT concerns the following property: _____
_____
_____   PRICE $ _____

In consideration of the mutual covenants and agreements herein contained, the undersigned Seller hereby gives to the undersigned Broker a non-exclusive agency to sell the said property for the price and on the terms and conditions herein set forth.

I.   The Broker agrees:
   a.   To use reasonable efforts to procure a ready, willing, and able Buyer of the property in accordance with the price, terms, and conditions of this Agreement.

II.   The Broker is granted the authority to: *(Check if applicable)*
   [ ] a.   Advertise the property;
   [ ] b.   Post "For Sale" signs on the property;
   [ ] c.   Cooperate with subagents; and/or
   [ ] d.   Offer compensation to buyer agents.
       (NOTE: Regardless of how compensated, buyer agents represent the interests of buyers, not sellers.)

III.   The Seller agrees:
   a.   To cooperate with the Broker in every reasonable way;
   b.   To pay the Broker a fee for professional services of _____ if the Broker procures a Buyer ready, willing, and able to buy said property, or any part thereof, in accordance with the price, terms and conditions of this Agreement, or such other price, terms and conditions as shall be acceptable to the Seller, whether or not the transaction proceeds.

   Once an offer has been accepted in writing and a transaction is pending, the Broker shall have no obligation to present further offers to the Seller.

IV.   The Seller understands and agrees that the property will be marketed in compliance with all applicable fair housing laws.

V.   The period of this Agreement shall be from _____, 199 ___, to and including
_____, 199 ___. Time is of the essence hereof.

Additional terms and conditions: _____
_____
_____

IN WITNESS WHEREOF, the Seller and the Broker have hereunto set their hands and seals as of the _____ day of
_____, 199 ____.

_____   _____
BROKER   SELLER

_____   _____
BROKER   SELLER
By_____

Its_____
    title (duly-authorized)

UNDER THE CODE OF ETHICS AND STANDARDS OF PRACTICE OF THE NATIONAL ASSOCIATION OF REALTORS®, ANY REALTOR® ENTERING INTO A LISTING CONTRACT MUST ADVISE THE SELLER OF

1. THE REALTOR'S® GENERAL COMPANY POLICIES REGARDING COOPERATION WITH SUBAGENTS, THE PAYMENT OF COMPENSATION TO BUYER AGENTS, OR BOTH;
2. THE FACT THAT BUYER AGENTS, EVEN IF COMPENSATED BY THE LISTING BROKER OR BY THE SELLER, WILL REPRESENT THE INTERESTS OF BUYERS; AND
3. ANY POTENTIAL FOR THE LISTING BROKER TO ACT AS A DISCLOSED DUAL AGENT ON BEHALF OF THE SELLER AS WELL AS THE BUYER.

Source: This form has been made available through the courtesy of the Greater Boston Real Estate Board, and is protected by the copyright laws.

Questions

1. A listing agreement:

   a. is an employment contract between a broker and the seller.
   b. is an agreement to purchase property signed by the buyer.
   c. must not specify a price for the property.
   d. may not state a specific commission.

2. Which type of listing agreement is illegal in Massachusetts?

   a. Open listing
   b. Net listing
   c. Exclusive-right-to-sell
   d. Exclusive agency listing

3. Which of the following agreements need *not* be in writing?

   a. Exclusive agency listing
   b. Open listing
   c. Exclusive-right-to-sell
   d. Multiple listing

4. Under which of the following may an owner *not* sell his or her home without a broker?

   a. Open listing
   b. Exclusive-right-to-sell
   c. Exclusive agency listing
   d. Multiple listing

5. Sally Seller told Bill Broker that she wanted $50,000 clear when she sold her house. Bill accepted the listing and sold it for $160,000. He gave $50,000 to Sally and kept the rest. Which of the following is correct?

   a. Bill should have given Sally a better appraisal of the value of her house.
   b. Bill's commission exceeds statutory and NAR guidelines.
   c. Bill accepted an illegal net listing.
   d. As Sally's agent, Bill had a duty to sell the house for as much as possible.

6. In a co-broker agreement,

   a. the finding broker shows a listing broker's property to a potential buyer.
   b. the finding broker may complete the transaction if he or she produces the buyer.
   c. the listing broker is the "cooperating broker."
   d. the listing broker divides the commission with the finding broker.

7. A "CMA" is a:

   a. comparative market appraisal.
   b. comparative marketing agreement.
   c. competitive market analysis.
   d. competitive market accounting.

8. The sales price of a house:

   a. is set by the selling broker in the listing agreement.
   b. should be based on a licensed broker's recommendation.
   c. is based on a licensed broker's appraisal.
   d. should be set by the seller.

9. Paula is buying a house near Springfield, using FHA financing. The appraisal may only be performed by:

   a. a licensed real estate broker.
   b. a licensed or certified real estate appraiser.
   c. any resident of Massachusetts.
   d. a comparative market analyst.

10. A broker may *not* do which of the following in regard to sales price?

    a. Give the seller advice.
    b. Provide information about comparable values.
    c. Express an opinion of what the proper selling price should be.
    d. Express concern about the seller's selected price

6

Interests in Real Estate

ESTATES IN LAND

When a valid deed is delivered, the law presumes that a fee simple estate has been conveyed with the delivery of the deed, unless the deed specifically states otherwise.

Legal Life Estates

Dower and Curtesy. The purpose underlying dower and curtesy is the protection of one spouse against disinheritance by the other. The original Massachusetts Dower and Curtesy Law provided that each spouse received a life estate in one-third of all lands owned by the other immediately upon their marriage. The wife's right is **dower**; the husband's is **curtesy**; both are often referred to collectively as "dower rights."

This traditional protection of spouses resulted in troubles for brokers: buyers could not get clear title to property unless both spouses signed the deed, and spouses were often estranged, missing, undisclosed, or unwilling to sign.

Under current law, a spouse's dower and curtesy rights are no longer effective on the wedding day, but rather at the moment of the other spouse's death. This permits transactions to be made during a spouse's lifetime by his or her signature alone. Dower and curtesy are still a life estate in one-third of the deceased spouse's real property.

Dower and curtesy rights are rarely exercised. Persons who are dissatisfied with their treatment under their deceased spouses' wills generally choose to exercise their waiver right under the Massachusetts Law of Descent and take the minimum statutory share of the estate (see Chapter 11). Further, because most married couples hold their property as tenants by the entirety or joint tenants, succession is not usually an issue. Only if an individual dies insolvent may dower or curtesy arise: the surviving spouse's right comes before the claims of creditors.

Homestead. The homestead right entitles a homeowner and his or her surviving spouse and minor children to a life estate of up to $125,000 in the land and buildings occupied as their principal residence. Disabled persons and those more than 62 years old are entitled to a homestead of $200,000. The purpose of homestead is to protect an individual's equity in his or her home. A declaration of homestead exempts certain property (land, buildings and manufactured homes) from the laws of conveyance, descent, devise, attachment, levy on execution, and sale for payment of debts up to the homestead value.

There are, naturally, some exceptions. In the case of bankruptcy, the homestead right available to all homeowners, regardless of age or condition, is limited to $50,000. Homestead will not prevent the enforcement of a lien for nonpayment of real estate taxes.

To acquire a homestead right, the deed of conveyance must include a statement or "declaration" that the principal residence will be held as a homestead. Homestead may also be invoked by recording a signed declaration in the Registry of Deeds for the county in which the land is located.

A homestead is exempt from sale for payment of all debts — with the following exceptions:

- First and second mortgages

- Probate court decrees for the support of a surviving spouse and minor children

- Unpaid federal, state and local taxes, assessments, claims and liens

- Debts contracted prior to the homestead declaration

- When buildings that do not belong to the holder of the homestead are attached or sold for the ground rent.

ENCUMBRANCES

Easements

There are three ways easements are commonly created in Massachusetts:

1. by deed;

2. by prescription; or

3. by necessity (implied easements).

Easement by Deed. An easement can be created by deed when a grantor (1) conveys a limited easement right to his or her property, or (2) conveys all his or her rights in a specific property but retains or reserves an easement. The grantor can use either a quitclaim or a warranty deed to create an easement (see Chapter 11). A *quitclaim deed* may be used to convey an easement when the grantor is conveying no other interest.

An easement may be granted for a specific, limited period of time to a specific individual, or to the grantee or his or her heirs and assignees forever.

Easement by Prescription. An easement by prescription is the equivalent of adverse possession. In Massachusetts, five factors must be established in order to establish an easement by prescription:

- 20 years of use or possession;

- continuous and uninterrupted use;

- use was without the owner's permission;

- the owner knew (or should have known) of the use, and took no action to prevent it; and

- a benefitted parcel of land, usually abutting or adjacent, must exist.

The final factor is intended to prevent the public from obtaining an easement. The 20-year period may include previous users of the easement.

FOR EXAMPLE ...

For the past 20 years, Jim has driven across his neighbor Fred's property several times a day in order to reach his garage from a more comfortable angle. Jim has an easement by prescription.

For 25 years, Lulu has driven across Fred's property two or three times a year to reach her property when she's in a hurry. She does not have an easement by prescription because her use was not continuous.

Twenty years ago, Edna arranged a line of colored stones marking the path she would like to use to cross Fred's property, but she never used the path. She does not have an easement.

For 15 years, Anna parked her car next to Fred's garage. Five years ago, she sold her house to Nick, who continued to park his car there. Nick now has a permanent easement by prescription.

But what if instead of parking his car by the garage, Nick simply recorded his easement in the county in which Fred's property is located? Nick would not have an easement, because recording documents or deeds does not, by itself, give notice to the owner.

Easement by Necessity. An easement by necessity is created when a seller conveys a parcel of land and the buyer has no way to reach the property except by crossing the seller's land or that of a neighboring owner. In determining whether or not an easement by necessity exists, courts will consider the intent of the parties at the time of the conveyance.

In particular, courts will consider:

- the specific geographic condition of the property (the "lay of the land");

- the buyer's and the seller's actual knowledge of the limited access; and

- references (or the absence of references) to an easement or right of access made in the conveyance document (deed).

This type of easement is not automatic, like the 20-year prescriptive easement. If a court determines that the parties did not intend an easement, none will be imposed. Nor will an easement be imposed if the grantee, by spending a reasonable amount of time and money, would be able to create another means of access to and from the property. Massachusetts courts consider each case on its own merits: there is no hard-line rule.

FOR EXAMPLE ...

Lou conveys a portion of his land to Bud. Bud's property is completely surrounded by Lou's land, with Road 1 separated from Bud's property by a rapidly-flowing river, and Road 2 on the other side of Lou's field. If the conveyance included an easement to the road, Bud would obviously have one. But if the conveyance expressly said "without any easement across Lou's property," Bud would not have an easement.

———————

In general, easements remain in effect against property and are not abandoned by nonuse. By statute and case law, however, the failure to re-record an easement at least once every 50 years can cause the easement to be unenforceable against a new owner of the property who has no knowledge of its existence. Usually, attorneys will restate or refer to easements in deeds as a title is transferred, giving notice of the continuing encumbrance.

License

A *license* is the smallest right a person can have in real estate. It arises out of a contract, not from a grant of ownership. A parking place, a hotel room and a movie seat are examples of licenses.

If a person rents parking space for a few hours, he or she has contracted for certain rights in the land: the right to park his or her car there, for instance, and the right to enter the property to recover the car. However, where the license is gratuitous — without payment or the underlying contractual elements — the license may be canceled without notice, and with no legal recourse for the licensee (the person who used the license).

FOR EXAMPLE ...

Herman's friend Ahab buys a boat in February. Ahab asks Herman for permission to leave the boat in Herman's backyard until the harbor opens in May. By permitting Ahab to store the boat on his property, Herman has given Ahab a license. But if Herman buys his own boat in March, he can tell Ahab to remove his boat, and Ahab will have no legal remedy.

———————

RIPARIAN RIGHTS

Owners of property that includes or lies alongside bodies of water face particular ownership issues, called *riparian rights*. In Massachusetts, there are three types of common riparian rights situations: streams, surface waters and tidal waters.

The word *riparian* refers to the rights of an owner along a river or watercourse, but when the rights are adjacent to a lake or the ocean they may be called *littoral* rights. The terms "riparian rights" and "riparian owner" are often used in conjunction with all water-related issues. For study purposes, just remember that *R*iparian refers to *R*ivers (and other flowing bodies of water), and *L*ittoral refers to *L*akes (and other surface waters).

Streams

If the stream is navigable — that is, if a boat can be floated down it — then the public owns both the water and the land under the water. The Commonwealth is responsible for the care and supervision of the stream. The owner of the land next to the stream, or through which the stream runs, owns the land *up to the bank* of the stream.

An owner of land abutting a navigable waterway owns the right to use the water as it passes, but he or she cannot obstruct it or prevent it from flowing in its natural course or from being used for navigation.

If the stream is nonnavigable, ownership may be held in one of two ways. If the stream separates two properties, the adjacent land-owners own the water and the land under the water to the center of the stream. If the stream runs through a single property, then the riparian owner owns the water all the way across and all the land on both sides and underneath.

Ponds and Lakes

Surface waters, such as ponds, swamps and lakes, are controlled by the state and are regulated according to antipollution statutes. Adjacent property owners own the land up to the shore and do not have an unlimited right to fill in a wetland or lakeshore. Use of the water must be approved under the state environmental laws.

Tidal Water

An owner whose property abuts tidal waters (that is, oceanfront property) owns the land to the mean low water line or 100 rods below mean high water, whichever is less. The land between low and high water is reserved for the use of the public by state law and is regulated by the state.

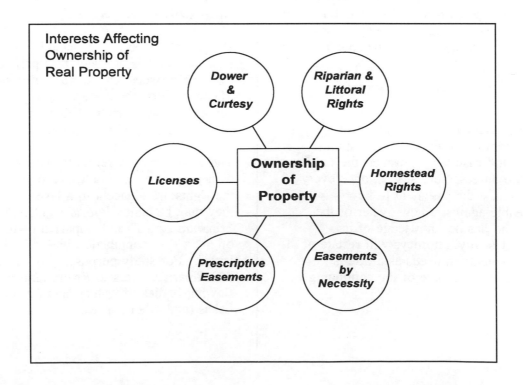

Interests Affecting Ownership of Real Property

Questions

1. When a valid deed is delivered, unless stated otherwise, it is assumed that which of the following estates is delivered?

   a. Life estate
   b. Leasehold
   c. Fee simple
   d. Freehold

2. In Massachusetts, dower and curtesy rights become effective:

   a. at the time of the marriage.
   b. at the moment of a spouse's death.
   c. when a creditor lays claim to the property.
   d. when the couple is divorced.

3. Which of the following statements is *not* true regarding the homestead right?

   a. The amount of the mortgage is exempt from the debt.
   b. The home must be the principal residence of the family.
   c. The homeowner, surviving spouse and minor children have a life estate.
   d. The homestead right does not have to be recorded.

4. *J* and *A* are married, and live in a home owned by *A*. When *J*'s wife died, *J* came into a life estate because of a(n):

   a. dower right.
   b. earned right.
   c. homestead right.
   d. curtesy right.

5. If an easement is to be acquired by prescription, it must be proved that which of the following is true?

   a. The owner's permission was given.
   b. The easement was used for 15 years.
   c. Only one person used the easement.
   d. There was a benefited parcel of land.

6. *L* sold the back half of his property to *M*. *L* wanted to grant *M* an easement so that *M* could use a strip of *L*'s land to get to the back half of *M*'s property. *L* should:

   a. have the easement written into the deed when title is conveyed.
   b. just tell Mike that he can drive across the strip.
   c. give Mike a notarized letter granting him permission to use the strip.
   d. let Mike use the strip for 20 years.

7. Which of the following statements about a license is *not* true?

   a. A license can be canceled without notice.
   b. A license is a grant of ownership.
   c. A license arises out of a contract.
   d. A licensee has purchased certain rights.

8. The smallest right that a person can have in real estate is a(n):

   a. license.
   b. life estate.
   c. lease.
   d. easement.

9. Littoral rights would be of interest to someone living in which of the following situations?

   a. On the bank of a river
   b. On the side of a hill
   c. On the edge of a forest.
   d. On an ocean beach.

10. If a river is navigable, the adjacent landowner owns the:

    a. land and water to the middle of the river.
    b. water in the river.
    c. land under the river.
    d. land to the bank of the river.

11. The purpose of homestead is to:

    a. protect spouses against disinheritance.
    b. ensure the payment of taxes, claims and liens.
    c. protect a person's equity in his or her home.
    d. permit a surviving spouse to retain the home.

12. Owners whose property is adjacent to a large pond own the:

    a. property to the shore, with their use of the water limited by environmental laws.
    b. property to the center of the pond, but may use the water only for recreation.
    c. property up to 100 rods from the shoreline,.
    d. entire pond if they agree to comply with the appropriate environmental regulations.

7

How Ownership Is Held

FORMS OF OWNERSHIP

Massachusetts recognizes tenancy in common, joint tenancy, tenancy by the entirety, and partnership ownership. Joint tenancy is discussed in the main text.

Tenancy in Common

In Massachusetts, it is presumed that when a deed conveys land to two or more people, it is conveying ownership as tenants in common, unless there is evidence that another form of ownership was intended.

Tenancy by the Entirety

A tenancy by the entirety is created when:

1. the conveying deed *expressly* transfers the property "to X and Y as tenants by the entirety"; and

2. the conveyance is to a *married couple*.

It is important to note that there must be an *express* statement that a tenancy by the entirety is being created — the mere fact that a property's owners are married does not automatically mean it is held by the entirety.

In Massachusetts, property is presumed to be held as tenants in common unless the deed explicitly states otherwise. A grant of land to two people who are not married, that specifies that they shall hold the land as tenants by the entirety will result in a joint tenancy.

An advantage of tenancies by the entirety created after February 1980 is that a creditor of either spouse cannot take action against property that is used as their home, because the ownership is indivisible. The disadvantage of this form of ownership, and the reason why some couples choose joint tenancy, is that neither individual may sell his or her share without destroying the tenancy by the entirety. A joint tenant may sell his or her share, and the purchaser becomes a tenant in common with the other joint tenant. In a tenancy by the entirety, however, the parties must be married to each other: conveying an interest to a non-marital party destroys the tenancy, creating a tenancy in common. Similarly, if a married couple divorces, a tenancy by the entirety converts to a tenancy in common. Just remember that this form of ownership is limited to two married persons who cannot convey or partition their interest without destroying the tenancy.

Because both husband and wife own the entire property, the surviving spouse will be the sole owner. If there is confusion in a deed about which estate is created by a husband and wife, but it is clear that a survivorship right is desired, courts will construe ownership as being a joint tenancy, not a tenancy by the entirety.

Partnership Ownership

Partnership ownership results if partnership funds are used in the purchase of property by persons who are partners. Massachusetts has adopted the Uniform Partnership Act, under the terms of which a partner may purchase property with partnership funds in his or her own individual name. The property does not have to be in the partnership's name.

COOPERATIVES, CONDOMINIUMS AND TIME-SHARES

Cooperative Housing Corporations

To foster the development of safe, decent and affordable housing, the state encourages the establishment of multiple-family housing cooperative associations. Following statutory requirements, a special kind of corporation is established in which each shareholder receives a *proprietary lease* entitling him or her to occupy a unit in the building and to the use of the common areas.

An individual in a cooperative association owns a *personal property interest* in the corporation that owns the building in which he or she lives.

Condominiums

Massachusetts has specific laws governing the conversion of existing rental property to condominium ownership. On both the state and local levels, these laws protect tenants who will be displaced by the sale of their property. The protections allow time for those who are dislocated to move or give the right of first refusal to purchase to present tenants. Some communities, faced with inadequate housing for low-income people, the elderly or the handicapped, have placed emergency moratoriums on condominium conversions.

Time-Share Ownership

Massachusetts has adopted the Model Real Estate Time-Share Act, which establishes uniform laws and procedures governing time-share estates.

In a time-share arrangement, a parcel is held by several owners in common. Each owner has the right to use the property for a certain period of time, which may be either fixed or variable. In Massachusetts, an ownership interest in a unit that includes the right of possession during a potentially infinite number of separate periods is an estate in fee simple, and includes all the rights of common law fee ownership. An interest in a unit that includes the right of possession during five or more separate time periods over a limited number of years that is greater than five, including extension and renewal options, is a common law estate for years. (See Chapter 6 in the main text for a discussion of fee simple estates and estates for years.)

Each time-share owner has financial responsibilities for the upkeep and preservation of the property. Although each interest represents a separate estate in real property, the time-share property is considered a single parcel for purposes of assessment and taxation. Owners pool their funds, and all fees and taxes are paid out from this pool. The Time-Share Act provides specific regulations for the sale, ownership and management of time-share properties.

There are numerous requirements governing how time-shares are created and offered. For example, a single property may be divided into more than 12 time-shares only by a recorded instrument that specifically describes the property, time periods, management provisions and the rights and liabilities of each time-share. The public offering statement advertising the availability of time-share units must contain detailed information about the property, the managing entity, the developer, and the time-share owner's rights and liabilities. If the promotional materials and time-share instrument promise improvements, the improvements must be made. If the time-share property is promoted through the use of prizes or other inducements, the approximate fair market value of the prize must be disclosed, along with how many are available and the criteria for winning.

Time-shares may be offered or sold in Massachusetts only by a "project broker" desig-nated by the time-share developer. The project broker must be a licensed real estate broker, and the time-share property is considered a separate real estate office for purposes of the license laws.

Quarter-share units are condominium units owned by four owners under a use agreement. Either method of sharing — time share or quarter share — is available by deed, lease or contract, and condominium laws apply.

Questions

1. Unless stated to the contrary in a deed, ownership of land by a married couple is assumed to be by:

   a. severalty.
   b. joint tenancy.
   c. tenancy in common.
   d. tenancy by the entirety.

2. *S* and *M* are married, and hold their property as tenants by the entirety. When *S* dies, *M* will:

   a. own one-half of the property.
   b. own a personal property interest.
   c. own a legal homestead interest.
   d. be sole owner of the property.

3. Which of the following forms of ownership represents a personal property interest?

   a. Tenancy by the entirety
   b. Partnership
   c. Tenancy in common
   d. Cooperative housing

4. In Massachusetts, a tenancy by the entirety:

   a. may be held only by husband and wife.
   b. continues after a spouse's death.
   c. may be partitioned.
   d. gives the husband control of the property.

5. *B* and *C* are a married couple living in Massachusetts. The deed to their property explicitly states that it is held as tenants by the entirety. In Massachusetts, they:

   a. automatically hold the property as joint tenants.
   b. own the property as tenants in common.
   c. may not hold the property as tenants by the entirety.
   d. hold the property as tenants by the entirety.

6. Which of the following is *not* recognized in Massachusetts?

   a. Tenancy in common
   b. Quarter-share
   c. Common property
   d. Tenancy by the entirety

7. Tenants of a building that is being converted to a condominium will:

   a. be given the right of first refusal.
   b. have to move.
   c. automatically become owners.
   d. be allowed to stay indefinitely.

8. Joan holds ownership in a cooperative building. She owns:

   a. in fee simple.
   b. in severalty.
   c. stock in a corporation.
   d. a partnership share.

9. Taxes on a time-share unit are:

   a. paid individually, by each owner.
   b. paid out of a common pool of funds.
   c. assessed against the board.
   d. paid only upon transfer.

10. Jack bought a condominium. When title is conveyed to Jack, he will:

    a. own his unit in fee simple.
    b. own stock in the association.
    c. pay his taxes to the board.
    d. not have to pay an assessment.

Legal Descriptions

METHODS OF DESCRIBING REAL ESTATE

Massachusetts does not use the rectangular survey system for the description of property. It has been impractical to attempt to change all existing metes-and-bounds descriptions, and the land is far too irregular in contour to allow such a system to function effectively.

In Massachusetts, the land is described by using what is known as a *full legal description*. The full legal description consists of three elements:

1. Street or designated *address* of the property involved

2. *Metes-and-bounds description*: a description of the location and length of the various boundaries, including the identification of ownership of adjacent tracts of land

3. *Reference description*: directs the reader to some other recorded document that gives greater definition of the location, shape and size of the property, such as a previous deed reference (by book, page and date); the plan or plat number from the Registry of Deeds; or a certificate number from the Land Court Records.

The use of the full legal description depends on a fixed set of boundary markers. Generally, each survey or description will begin at a *monument*, sometimes called a *benchmark*, which is a fixed, permanent marker. Then the description proceeds around the property, going from monument to monument. In Massachusetts, monuments are commonly iron pipes, granite blocks, trees, boulders, walls, telephone poles or buildings.

Many monuments that seemed fixed and permanent at one time have moved, changed, or become lost over a period of years. This has made a current survey almost mandatory in many land transactions, and the broker should find out who in the area is qualified to conduct such a survey. While a current survey is not essential, without one the buyer never really knows what he or she is buying. A survey *must* be ordered and a plat obtained when the property will be subdivided. The top of a plat is usually considered to be north, and it is customary for the direction north to be indicated by an arrow.

Although it is possible to use fewer than all three of these elements to describe land in a contract, real estate brokers and salespersons should make every effort to ensure that the full legal description is used in all real estate documents. It should also be noted that, in a deed, a street address, standing alone, is not a sufficient description of a parcel of land, and would not be acceptable as the sole description in a deed.

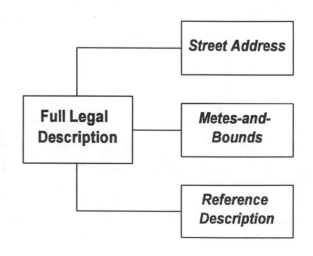

Figure 8.1   Plat of Honeysuckle Hills Subdivision

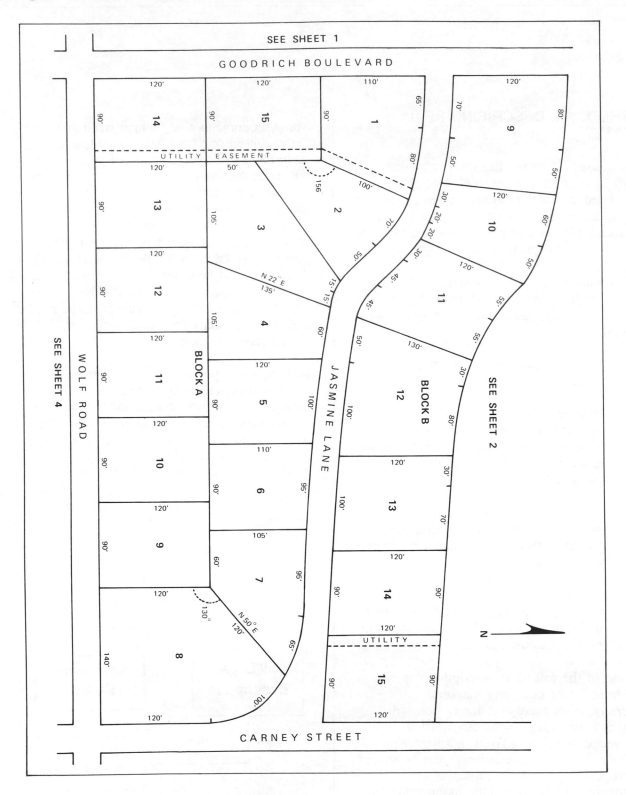

Questions

1. Which of the following is *not* an adequate description of land in a deed?

   a. Street address
   b. Metes-and-bounds description
   c. Reference description
   d. Street address and metes and bounds description

2. A metes-and-bounds description will:

   a. return to the point of beginning.
   b. refer to some other recorded plan.
   c. have four sides.
   d. include a street address.

3. The data for a metes-and-bounds description is created by a:

   a. landowner.
   b. bank attorney.
   c. licensed surveyor.
   d. broker.

Answer the following questions according to the plat of Honeysuckle Hills in Figure 8.1.

4. Which lot in Block B has the most frontage on Jasmine Lane?

   a. Lot 9   c. Lot 12
   b. Lot 13   d. Lot 11

5. How many lots have easements?

   a. 3   c. 4
   b. 1   d. None

6. Which roads run north and south?

   a. Goodrich and Jasmine
   b. Wolf and Jasmine
   c. Carney and Goodrich
   d. Goodrich and Wolf

7. Which lot in the subdivision has the least frontage on Jasmine Lane?

   a. Block B, Lot 11   c. Block B, Lot 12
   b. Block A, Lot 4   d. Block A, Lot 3

8. "Beginning at the intersection of the East line of Goodrich Boulevard and the South line of Jasmine Lane and running South along the East line of Goodrich Boulevard a distance of 230 feet: thence East parallel to the North line of Wolfe Road a distance of 195 feet: thence Northeasterly on a course N 22° E a distance of 135 feet: and thence Northwesterly along the South line of Jasmine Lane to the point of beginning."

   Which lots are described here?

   a. Lots 13, 14 and 15, Block A
   b. Lots 9, 10 and 11, Block B
   c. Lots 1, 2, 3 and 15, Block A
   d. Lots 7, 8 and 9, Block A

9. Which lot has the most street exposure?

   a. Lot 15   c. Lot 8
   b. Lot 14   d. Lot 9

10. Assume that the bold number "15" in the middle of Lot 15 represents the location of a *monument*. The monument marks the southeast corner of a subdivided parcel. If the parcel is bounded by Goodrich and Lot 1, approximately how many square feet is the subdivided parcel?

    a. 1,210 square feet   c. 4,500 square feet
    b. 2,700 square feet   d. 5,400 square feet

Real Estate Taxes and Other Liens

LIENS

Massachusetts Real Estate Taxes

Each town and city in the state is responsible for raising revenue through a property tax. The tax year begins January 1, although for budgeting and appropriation purposes a community may use the fiscal year from July 1 to the following June 30.

The purpose of real estate taxes is to fund a community's budget. Once the spending plan has been decided, the community must determine how to most fairly distribute the cost of programs and services among property owners. All property within a community is assessed at the same time, at 100 percent of its fair market value. Then the amount of the community's budget that will be raised from real estate taxes is divided by the total of all the assessed values. The result is the amount of the budget each dollar's worth of property will bear, generally quoted as X dollars per $1,000 of assessed value.

FOR EXAMPLE ...

The town of Bedford Falls has an annual budget of $300,000. There are fifty property owners in the town, and each property has an assessed fair market value of $75,000. To determine the real estate tax, perform the following calculation:

300,000 ÷ ($75,000 x 50 = $3,750,000) = 0.08

$0.08 is the amount each owner must pay for every dollar's worth of property he or she owns. So, each owner must pay $80 per $1,000 assessed value, or $6,000 in real estate taxes.

The annual real estate tax bills are prepared and sent out before October 1. While the tax is payable on November 1, a taxpayer may choose to pay only one-half on that date and the other half on May 1. Bills for improvements made by the municipality are due annually on November 1.

It should be noted that "Proposition 2½," passed in 1978, limits property taxes throughout Massachusetts to 2.5 percent of assessed value. Because the cap may adversely effect tax-dependent bodies such as schools and emergency services, individual communities may vote to override it.

Unpaid Real Estate Taxes

Real estate taxes that remain unpaid two years after they are due may be collected by a tax sale of the property. Because the owner has one year from the date of the tax sale to redeem the property, called a *right of redemption*, the purchaser of a tax deed cannot be assured of acquiring title. If no redemption is made within two years from the date of the tax sale, the new owner can bring an action in the land court to register the title and confirm ownership. Land court registration and the Torrens system are described in Chapter 12.

Other Liens

Municipal Liens. Municipal liens on a property may be ascertained by checking the records at the Registry of Deeds for the county in which the land is located, or by securing a municipal lien certificate from the local tax collector. The lien certificate indicates unpaid real estate taxes, water charges, betterments, assessments and other unpaid or current financial obligations levied by the town or city against the land.

Mechanic's Lien. If a person supplies labor involved in the erection, alteration, repair or removal of a building or structure on the land because of an agreement or contract with the owner of the property, the person supplying the labor has a lien against the land. If a subcontractor provides labor and materials through a contract, the subcontractor has a right to claim a lien, even if the landowner paid the contractor and the contractor failed to pay the subcontractor. The subcontractor has a right to the lien, based on the date when he or she finished the work. The lien will protect the value of up to 18 days of work that was actually supplied during the 40 days prior to the filing of a lien at the Registry of Deeds. Liens are generally given priority based on the date and time of filing.

If the contractor is working under a written contract with the owner, the contractor has 30 days in which to file a notice of a lien; if notice is filed, the lien may be enforced prior to the completion of the contract. By using this provision of the law, persons may be protected should a dispute arise over who is obligated to pay the bill for services rendered.

From the owner's point of view, the mechanic's lien provides an obstacle that should be circumvented by using release forms that relieve the owner from claims by subcontractors in the event the contractor fails to pay them. A high risk of claims -- and clouds on a property's title -- exists without the use of releases.

Title 5 Betterments. Most title transfers in Massachusetts now require a "Title 5 inspection" of on-site sewage disposal systems. If the existing system is found to be deficient, the homeowner must repair or upgrade the system to meet environmental standards (see Appendix).

The Massachusetts legislature has created a $10 million long-term loan program to assist homeowners who lack sufficient funds to have the Title 5 repair or upgrade work performed. The loan appears as a betterment assessment on the tax bill — similar to the way sidewalks or street improvements appear. The presence of such an assessment has led some banks to refuse mortgages for homes subject to Title 5 assessments.

Questions

1. Property taxes are assessed and collected by:

   a. individual municipalities.
   b. the county where the property is located.
   c. the state tax officer.
   d. the land court.

2. Property in Massachusetts must be reassessed at:

   a. 80 percent of the market value.
   b. 60 percent of the market value.
   c. 100 percent of the market value.
   d. 90 percent of the market value.

3. If there is no redemption of the property, how long must a tax sale purchaser wait before starting action to obtain title to the land?

   a. Two years after the unpaid taxes are due.
   b. One year from the date of the tax sale.
   c. Three years from the date of the tax sale.
   d. Two years from the date of the tax sale.

4. To acquire title to the land, a tax sale purchaser:

   a. registers the deed to the property at the Registry of Deeds.
   b. files a tax certificate with the Registry of Deeds.
   c. brings action in the land court to register title and confirm ownership.
   d. pays the back taxes and file a tax release at the Registry of Deeds.

5. To ensure that a property is free from municipal liens, the attorney for the purchaser will obtain a municipal lien certificate from:

   a. the local tax collector.
   b. the Registry of Deeds.
   c. the state tax office.
   d. the local courthouse.

6. How long does an owner have to redeem property sold for back taxes?

   a. 1 year   c. 40 days
   b. 2 years   d. 18 months

7. The Browns have hired a general contractor, Shoddy Construction Co., to remodel their kitchen. To avoid a mechanic's lien on the property, they should:

   a. have Shoddy promise to pay the subcontractors.
   b. file a lis pendens.
   c. pay the subcontractors directly.
   d. obtain release forms from Shoddy.

8. Assuming they all provided exactly the service implied by their name, which of the following parties would *not* be entitled to a mechanic's lien against the Browns' property?

   a. Sure-Amic Kitchen Tile Installation Co.
   b. Counter-Culture Countertops, Inc.
   c. Cool's Refrigerator Sales Store
   d. Plenty-o-Plumbing Co.

9. In question 8, *why* was the party not entitled to a mechanic's lien?

   a. Because kitchen tile is not a fixture
   b. Because the general contractor is responsible for paying subcontractors
   c. Because selling a refrigerator is not performing labor on the property
   d. Because plumbing becomes a fixture

10. A subcontractor worked for 22 days on a project, at a daily cost of $500. The contractor failed to pay the subcontractor, who properly filed a lien 33 days after work was completed. What is the value of the work protected by the lien?

    a. $9,000   c. $16,500
    b. $11,000   d. $500

Real Estate Contracts

CONTRACT LAW

In Massachusetts, a contract for the sale of real estate must be in writing. The Statute of Frauds requires a written memorandum that includes:

- the identity of the parties;

- a description of the property;

- a recital of the consideration;

- the date of the agreement; and

- the signatures of the parties.

The signatures of both parties always should be obtained, because a party cannot be sued for any breach of a contract unless the contract has been signed. Any contract reduced to writing must be a complete document and include all the terms of the agreement. The Statute of Frauds' requirements represent only the bare minimum. From a practical standpoint, brokers are not properly fulfilling their obligation to the principal or being attentive to their own interest if a complete and legally enforceable contract is not prepared and executed.

Legally competent parties. In Massachusetts, a person becomes of age and can be held responsible for his or her contracts upon reaching 18 years of age.

Broker's Authority to Prepare Documents

In Massachusetts, a broker may complete a real estate sales contract. However, real estate brokers do not need to have a detailed knowledge of legal documents: many pre-

printed forms, such as offers to purchase and purchase and sale agreements, are available from stationery companies, the Massachusetts Association of Real Estate Boards and regional real estate boards. (See Figures 10.1 through 10.4.) Real estate brokers and salespersons who are not licensed attorneys must not attempt to draft legal documents.

Sales Contracts

Earnest money deposits. Massachusetts license law requires brokers to deposit earnest money and other customer's monies "in a separate bank account maintained by the broker." The account should be outside the reach of a broker's creditors. Some buyers and sellers request that the earnest money be put in an interest-bearing account. It is important that this be stated in the purchase and sale agreement and that it be clearly indicated who will receive the interest.

A real estate broker or agent's responsibilities regarding the handling of others' funds are discussed in Chapter 13.

Equitable title. When a buyer and seller sign a contract for the sale of real estate located in Massachusetts, the buyer immediately becomes the *equitable owner*. This does not give the buyer actual legal ownership of the property, but it gives what a court would recognize as an equitable interest. That is, the buyer has the right to become the owner, or the right to have the title transferred.

Liquidated damages. Most contracts in Massachusetts contain a liquidated damages clause that permits the seller to retain all or part of the earnest money deposit as liquidated damages in the event of the buyer's default.

Usually, the clause in the contract reads:

Should the buyer default, the seller and the broker may divide the earnest money deposit equally as liquidated damages.

The amount of liquidated damages must reasonably approximate what the damage might be; if the amount is excessive, the court will view it as a penalty and will not allow the seller to keep the entire amount.

Liquidated damages are a mixed bag for all parties. The benefit to buyers of having a liquidated damages clause in the contract is that their liability is defined and limited. On the other hand, buyers are guaranteed a loss in the event they breach the contract for any reason. While including a liquidated damages clause sometimes means that the seller gives up the right to sue for any actual damages, he or she is assured of compensation for the time the property was unnecessarily held off the market. In some contracts, however, the seller is entitled to take the liquidated damages *and* pursue other remedies against the buyer, including specific performance. Brokers give up the right to sue the seller for a total commission, but are entitled to some compensation for the lost income.

Reciprocal liquidated damages clauses based on seller default are rare. Normally, in the event of a seller default, the buyer would seek specific performance, sue for actual damages or simply demand return of the deposit.

Installment Contracts

Under an installment contract, the seller retains legal title to the property until the entire purchase price is paid, usually over a term of many years. Often the seller finances the purchase, and the buyer sends the seller monthly checks until the entire amount, including interest, is paid.

If the seller becomes insolvent during the term of the contract, the seller's creditors may attach and dispose of any property held in the seller's name, including the property the buyer is purchasing. This leaves the buyer of the property in no better position than a creditor. In many cases, however, a properly recorded equitable ownership can give the buyer a claim to the property, and creditors are limited to attaching the seller's right to receive the payments. In any event, this can be a dangerous method of purchasing property if the buyer does not obtain proper legal counsel. Installment contracts are seldom used in Massachusetts.

Figure 10.1   Offer to Purchase Real Estate

**FOR RESIDENTIAL PROPERTY CONSTRUCTED PRIOR TO 1978,
BUYER(S) MUST ALSO SIGN LEAD PAINT
"PROPERTY TRANSFER NOTIFICATION CERTIFICATION"**

From the Office of:

OFFER TO PURCHASE REAL ESTATE

TO _____
            (Seller and Spouse)
_____
_____   Date _____

The property herein referred to is identified as follows: ....
....
Special provisions (if any) re fixtures, appliances, etc.: ....
....
....
I hereby offer to buy said property, which has been offered to me by _____
_____ as the Seller's Broker(s) under the following terms and conditions:
                                                                        CHECK ONE:
1. I will pay therefore $ _____, of which   ☐ Check, subject to collection
   (a) $ .... is paid herewith as a deposit to bind this Offer   ☐ Cash
   (b) $ .... is to be paid as an additional deposit upon the execution of the Purchase and Sale Agreement provided for below.
   (c) $ .... is to be paid at the time of delivery of the Deed in cash, or by certified, cashier's, treasurer's or bank check(s).
   (d) $ ....
       _____
   (e) $ .... Total Purchase Price
2. This Offer is good until _____ A.M. P.M. on _____ 19_____ at or before which time a copy hereof shall be signed by you, the Seller and your (husband) (wife), signifying acceptance of this Offer, and returned to me forthwith, otherwise this Offer shall be considered as rejected and the money deposited herewith shall be returned to me forthwith.
3. The parties hereto shall, on or before _____ A.M. P.M. _____ 19_____ execute the applicable Standard Form Purchase and Sale Agreement recommended by the Greater Boston Real Estate Board or any form substantially similar thereto, which, when executed, shall be the agreement between the parties hereto.
4. A good and sufficient Deed, conveying a good and clear record and marketable title shall be delivered at 12:00 Noon on _____ 19_____, at the appropriate Registry of Deeds, unless some other time and place are mutually agreed upon in writing.
5. If I do not fulfill my obligations under this Offer, the above mentioned deposit shall forthwith become your property without recourse to either party. Said deposit shall be held by _____ as escrow agent subject to the terms hereof, provided however that in the event of any disagreement between the parties, the escrow agent may retain said deposit pending instructions mutually given by the parties. A similar provision shall be included in the Purchase and Sale Agreement with respect to any deposits held under its terms.
6. Time is of the essence hereof.
7. The initialed riders, if any, attached hereto are incorporated herein by reference. Additional terms and conditions, if any:
   ....
   ....
   ....

NOTICE: This is a legal document that creates binding obligations. If not understood, consult an attorney.

WITNESS my hand and seal.   SIGNED _____
                                                          Buyer
                                             _____
                                             Buyer   (home)
                                                                      (work)
Address   Phone Numbers
This Offer is hereby accepted upon the foregoing terms and conditions at _____ A.M./P.M. on _____ 19_____
    WITNESS my (our) hand(s) and seal(s).

_____   _____
Seller (or spouse)   Seller

RECEIPT FOR DEPOSIT
_____ 19_____

Received from _____ Buyer the sum of $ _____ as deposit under the terms

and conditions of above Offer, to be held by _____ as escrow agent.

**Under regulations adopted pursuant to the Massachusetts license law,
"all offers obtained by brokers or salesmen on any properties listed
with them shall be forthwith conveyed to the owner of said real estate."**

_____
                                             Agent for Seller

Source: This form has been made available through the courtesy of the Greater Boston Real Estate Board and is protected by the copyright laws.

Figure 10.2   Offer to Purchase Real Estate

OFFER TO PURCHASE REAL ESTATE

Date: _____ , 19 _____

The BUYER offers to _____ (SELLER) to buy the property with buildings and improvements thereon, located at _____ , in _____ ; Ma., which the BUYER viewed on _____ , 19___ . The property was offered for sale at $ _____ .

1. The BUYER offers to pay $ _____ for the property as follows:
   (a) $ _____ is paid as a deposit to bind this offer.
   (b) $ _____ is to be paid as an additional deposit upon the execution of a Purchase and Sale Agreement as provided below.
   (c) $ _____ is the balance to be paid on the closing date of on or before _____ , 19___ .

2. This offer is subject to the following conditions:
   (a) The BUYER's ability to obtain a (conventional, FHA, VA, MHFA, etc.) _____ mortgage in the amount of $ _____ by _____ , 19___ at prevailing rates.
   (b) Inspections(s) of the property satisfactory to the BUYER at the BUYER'S expense.
   (c) The execution of a Purchase and Sale Agreement for the property which shall then become the agreement between the parties no later than _____ , 19___ . If a Purchase and Sale Agreement has not been executed within the time specified, this offer shall become null and void and all payments hereunder shall be refunded and all obligations of the parties to each other shall cease.
   (d) Other provisions.

3. This offer is good through _____ , 19___ on or before which time this offer shall be signed by the SELLER signifying the acceptance or rejection of this offer and returned to the BUYER without delay.

NOTICE: This is a legal document that creates certain binding obligations.

_____   _____
BUYER   BUYER

I have informed the above-named BUYER[S] that I am a:	☐ Seller's Agent ☐ Buyer's Agent ☐ Disclosed Dual Agent
_____ Signature of Real Estate Agent	_____ Company

ACCEPTANCE: THIS OFFER IS HEREBY ACCEPTED.

_____   _____   _____
SELLER   DATE   SELLER   DATE   Broker

REJECTION: THIS OFFER IS HEREBY REJECTED.

_____   _____   _____
SELLER   DATE   SELLER   DATE   Broker

Rev. 11/93

Source: This form has been made available through the courtesy of the Greater Springfield Association of REALTORS®, and is protected by the copyright laws.

Figure 10.3   Purchase and Sale Agreement

PURCHASE AND SALE AGREEMENT

1. PARTIES. This Agreement is made this   day of   , 19

between

                                                         hereinafter called the SELLER,

and

                                                         hereinafter called the BUYER.

2. DESCRIPTION.   Subject to the terms and conditions hereinafter set forth, the SELLER agrees to sell and the BUYER agrees to buy

the following bounded and described premises:

as more particularly described in a Deed dated   ,19   and recorded in the   County

Registry of Deeds in Book   Page   or Land Court Certificate #

3. BUILDINGS, STRUCTURES, IMPROVEMENTS, FIXTURES.   Included in the sale as part of said premises are all buildings, structures, improvements and fixtures located in or on the premises belonging to the SELLER and used in connection therewith including, IF ANY, all venetian blinds, curtain rods, window shades, wall to wall carpeting, screen doors, storm windows and doors, awnings, shutters, furnaces, heaters, oil and gas burners and fixtures appurtenant thereto, hot water tanks, plumbing fixtures, electrical and other lighting fixtures, TV antennas, rotors and controls, garage door openers and controls, mantels, fences, gates, trees, shrubs, plants, and, IF BUILT-IN, exhaust fans, garbage disposers, dishwashers, air conditioning equipment, incinerators, kitchen ranges and ovens, and vacuum cleaners.
Items to be transferred to the BUYER in "as is" condition and not to be considered part of the sale are:

(if none, state "none") _____

Not included in the sale as part of the premises are the following items:

(if none, state "none") _____

Not included in the sale as part of the premises are the following rented fixtures not belonging to the SELLER:

(if none, state "none") _____

4. TITLE. Said premises are to be conveyed on or before   ,19   by a good and sufficient Deed of the SELLER which shall be a Deed of equal character and covenants as held by the SELLER, conveying a good, clear record and marketable title to the same free from all encumbrances, except:
  a. Usual public utilities servicing the premises, if any;
  b. Taxes for the current year not due and payable on the date of delivery of the Deed;
  c. Any liens for municipal assessments and/or orders for which assessments may be made after the date of this Agreement;
  d. Restrictions and easements of record, if any, which do not materially affect the value or current use
     (single family and/or   ) of the premises;
  e. Provisions of existing building and zoning laws.

5. CONSIDERATION. For such Deed and conveyance the BUYER is to pay the sum of.................. PRICE $
of which..DEPOSIT $
have been paid this day as a deposit and... BALANCE DUE $
are to be paid in cash, or by certified or bank check upon delivery of the Deed.

6. PERFORMANCE. The Deed is to be delivered and the consideration paid at the Registry of Deeds in which the Deed should be by law recorded on   ,19   at   M, unless some other place and time should be mutually agreed upon. To enable the SELLER to make conveyance as herein provided, the SELLER may, at the time of delivery of the Deed, use the purchase money or any portion thereof to clear the title of any and all encumbrances or interests; and all instruments so procured to clear the title shall be recorded simultaneously with the delivery of the Deed.

1

REV. 10/93   COPYRIGHT© 1993 GREATER SPRINGFIELD ASSOCIATION OF REALTORS®, INC.

Source: This form has been made available through the courtesy of the Greater Springfield Association of REALTORS®, and is protected by the copyright laws.

Figure 10.3   Purchase and Sale Agreement   (Continued)

7. CASUALTY LOSS. In case of any damage to the premises by fire or other casualty after the signing and delivery of this Agreement by all parties hereto, and unless the premises shall have been restored to its former condition by the SELLER prior to the performance date, the BUYER may, at the BUYER'S option, either cancel this Agreement and recover all sums paid hereunder or require as part of this Agreement that the SELLER pay over or assign, on delivery of the Deed, all sums recovered or recoverable on any and all insurance covering such damage.

8. POSSESSION. Full possession of the premises, free of all tenants and occupants, except the tenants as provided hereinbelow, is to be delivered to the BUYER at the time of the delivery of the Deed, the said premises to be then in the same condition in which they now are, reasonable use and wear of the buildings thereon excepted. The SELLER also agrees that the premises will be delivered to the BUYER in "broom clean" condition. The BUYER shall have the right to inspect the premises for compliance with this paragraph prior to delivery of the Deed upon reasonable notice to the SELLER'S Broker.

9. ADJUSTMENTS. Fuel, rents, security and rent deposits and any interest due thereon, water rates, sewer use and taxes shall be apportioned as of the day of delivery of the Deed. If the amount of said taxes is not known at the time of the delivery of the Deed, they shall be apportioned on the basis of the taxes assessed for the preceding year with a reapportionment as soon as the new tax rate and valuation can be ascertained, which latter provision shall survive the delivery of the Deed.

10. DEPOSITS. All deposits made hereunder shall be held by   herein called the SELLER'S Broker, as agent for the SELLER and shall be duly accounted for at the time for performance of this Agreement. In the event of a dispute between SELLER, BUYER, and/or Broker[s] as to any or all of the provisions of this Agreement or the performance thereof, the SELLER'S Broker shall retain all deposits hereunder in the SELLER'S Broker's escrow account, unless some other agreement is reached in writing between the parties, or until the dispute is resolved either by court judgment or by binding settlement between the parties. In the event that the SELLER'S Broker is made a party to any lawsuit by virtue of acting as escrow agent, the SELLER'S Broker shall be entitled to recover reasonable attorney's fees and costs, which fees and costs may be deducted from escrowed funds. Such fees and costs shall be assessed as court costs in favor of the prevailing party.

11. PROFESSIONAL SERVICES. A fee of   is to be paid by the SELLER to the SELLER'S Broker at time of delivery of the Deed.

A fee of   is to be paid by the BUYER to the BUYER'S Broker at time of delivery of the Deed.

12. BROKER AS A PARTY. The Broker[s] join in this Agreement and become parties hereto, insofar as any provisions of this Agreement expressly apply to the Broker[s] and to any amendments or modifications of such provisions to which the Broker[s] agree in writing.

13. DEFAULT. If the BUYER shall default under this Agreement, the BUYER shall forfeit the BUYER'S deposits and the SELLER'S Broker shall deliver the deposits to the SELLER. In addition to forfeiting the deposits, the BUYER shall be liable to the SELLER for any damages incurred by the SELLER as a result of the BUYER'S default.

14. MORTGAGE CONTINGENCY. This Agreement is contingent on the BUYER'S ability to obtain a   mortgage loan commitment of $. If, despite the BUYER's diligent efforts, a commitment for such loan cannot be obtained on or before   , 19   , the BUYER shall so advise the SELLER'S Broker in writing and this Agreement shall become null and void, and all payments made hereunder shall be refunded and all obligations to each other shall cease. If such written notice is not received on or before the expiration date hereinabove specified, the BUYER shall be bound to perform the BUYER'S obligations under this Agreement. Further, the BUYER agrees to provide such reasonable documentation of the BUYER's failure to obtain such loan commitment as the SELLER may request. In no event shall the BUYER be deemed to have used "diligent efforts" to obtain such commitment unless the BUYER submits a complete mortgage loan application conforming to the foregoing provisions forthwith.

15. SMOKE DETECTORS. The SELLER shall provide to the BUYER at the time of delivery of the Deed a certificate from the fire department certifying that the premises conform to Massachusetts General Laws, Chapter 148, Section 26F, concerning approved smoke detectors.

16. TERMITE INSPECTION. This Agreement is subject to the right of the BUYER to obtain, at BUYER'S own expense, a termite or other wood destroying insect inspection and written report being made by a recognized exterminator on or before the date hereinafter set forth. If the inspection shows that there is no evidence of termite or other wood destroying infestation in the existing construction or if infestations had existed, they have been corrected, this Agreement shall be in full force. If the inspection shows there is evidence of termites or other wood destroying infestations, and/or damage as a result of infestations, the BUYER shall furnish the SELLER'S Broker with a copy of the written reports stating the results of the inspection. If said inspection reveals that there is infestation and that it should be treated or that any damage caused thereby requires repair, and the total cost of treatment and repair does not exceed $1,000.00, the SELLER shall undertake such treatment and/or repair and the BUYER shall be bound to perform the BUYER'S obligations under this Agreement. In the event that said cost shall exceed $1,000.00, the BUYER, at BUYER'S option, may bear all expense in excess of $1,000.00, or may cancel this Agreement by notifying the SELLER'S Broker in writing upon receipt of such written report; in said event, this Agreement shall become null and void and all deposits made hereunder shall be refunded to the BUYER. If such written reports are not received on or before the inspection expiration date as set forth in paragraph 21, the BUYER shall be bound to perform BUYER'S obligations under this Agreement.

Figure 10.3   Purchase and Sale Agreement   (Continued)

17. UREA-FORMALDEHYDE FOAM INSULATION. The SELLER hereby discloses to the BUYER that the premises does _____ does not _____ contain Urea-Formaldehyde Foam Insulation ("UFFI"). If the premises contains UFFI, the BUYER acknowledges that the SELLER has, prior to the signing of this Agreement, delivered to the BUYER (a) the written UFFI Disclosure Statement required by applicable law, (b) a copy of the test results obtained by the SELLER pertaining to the formaldehyde gas levels, if any, in the premises and (c) a copy of information developed by the Department of Public Health relating to formaldehyde levels associated with the presence or absence of UFFI in dwellings.

18. LEAD PAINT LAW. The BUYER acknowledges that under Massachusetts Law, whenever a child under six (6) years of age resides in any premises in which paint, plaster or other accessible material contains dangerous levels of lead, the owner of said premises must remove or cover said material so as to make it inaccessible to children under six (6) years of age. The BUYER further acknowledges that prior to the signing of this Agreement, the SELLER and the Broker[s] have (a) provided to the BUYER the standard notification form from the Massachusetts Department of Public Health concerning lead paint and the BUYER signed the property transfer notification certificate; (b) disclosed to the BUYER any information known to the SELLER or the Broker[s] or any of them about the presence of such materials containing dangerous levels of lead in the premises; (c) informed the BUYER of the availability of inspections for dangerous levels of lead; and (d) verbally informed the BUYER of the possible presence of dangerous levels of lead and the provisions of the lead paint law and regulations.

19. UNDERGROUND STORAGE TANKS. The parties acknowledge that the Massachusetts Board of Fire Prevention has issued regulations governing the maintenance, repair and removal of underground storage tanks to prevent and detect leakage of tank contents into surrounding soil and water supplies. The SELLER hereby discloses that there are ___ are not ___ underground storage tank(s) at the premises. If there are one or more underground tanks at the premises, the SELLER further discloses that the tank(s) have___ have not___ been used within the past six (6) months exclusively for the storage of fuel oil for consumption on the premises and to the best of the SELLER'S knowledge there has been no release or leaking of oil from such tank(s). In the event that such tanks have not been so used, SELLER agrees that SELLER will comply with the applicable provisions of 527 CMR 9.00 et seq. regarding the removal/filling of such tanks so that at the time of the delivery of the Deed, the premises will be in compliance with the provisions of the aforesaid regulations.

20. MISCELLANEOUS REPRESENTATIONS.

    a. In the event that a private water source is servicing the premises, the SELLER represents that the water source is providing adequate amounts of potable water for normal household use as of the date hereof.

    b. In the event that a private sewerage system is servicing the premises, the SELLER represents that, to the best of the SELLER'S knowledge, it is in good working order as of the date hereof.

    c. The SELLER represents that all mechanical components will be in operating condition at the time of delivery of the Deed, unless otherwise stipulated in this Agreement.

21. RIGHT TO INSPECT; ACKNOWLEDGEMENT. This Agreement is subject to the right of the BUYER to obtain, at BUYER'S own expense, an inspection of the premises and written report to include, but not be limited to, the structural condition of the dwelling(s), pool(s) if any, other structures if any, the condition of all systems in the dwelling(s) or on the premises, the existence and condition of underground storage tanks if any, the presence of insect infestation, the presence of hazardous materials on the premises or the likelihood of release of hazardous materials on or from the premises, the presence of asbestos, urea-formaldehyde foam insulation, lead based paint and/or radon gas, the adequacy and suitability of the water supply and the condition and adequacy of the sewerage system. by the consultant(s) of the BUYER'S own choosing. The BUYER's right of inspection shall expire on _____ ,19 (recommended 10 days). The BUYER and the BUYER'S consultant(s) shall have the right of access to the premises at reasonable times upon twenty four (24) hours advance notice to the SELLER'S Broker, for the purpose of inspecting, as aforesaid the condition of said premises. If the BUYER is not satisfied with the results of such inspection(s), except as provided in paragraph 16, this Agreement may be terminated by the BUYER, at the BUYER's election, without legal or equitable recourse to either party, the parties thereby releasing each other from all liability under this Agreement, and the deposit shall be returned to the BUYER, provided however, that the BUYER shall have notified the SELLER'S Broker, in writing, together with a copy of the written report(s) of the inspection(s) on or before the inspection expiration date hereinabove specified, of the BUYER'S intention to so terminate. If such notice and written report(s) are not received on or before the inspection expiration date hereinabove specified, the BUYER shall be bound to perform BUYER'S obligations under this Agreement.

BUYER ACKNOWLEDGES THAT: (a) INFORMATION WAS SUPPLIED BY THE SELLER AND HAS NOT BEEN CHECKED FOR ACCURACY BY THE SELLER'S BROKER; (b) PUBLIC INFORMATION WAS SUBJECT TO BUYER'S VERIFICATION; (c) EACH ITEM WAS SUBJECT TO DIRECT INQUIRY BY THE BUYER, AND THE BUYER HAS BEEN SO ADVISED; (d) THE SELLER'S BROKER MAKES NO REPRESENTATIONS REGARDING THE CONDITION OF THE PREMISES, STRUCTURE(S) THEREON OR THE MECHANICAL COMPONENTS THEREOF; AND (e) THE BUYER HAS NOT BEEN INFLUENCED TO ENTER INTO THIS AGREEMENT NOR HAS THE BUYER RELIED UPON ANY WARRANTIES OR REPRESENTATIONS NOT SET FORTH OR INCORPORATED IN THIS AGREEMENT OR PREVIOUSLY MADE IN WRITING, EXCEPT FOR THE FOLLOWING ADDITIONAL WARRANTIES OR REPRESENTATIONS, IF ANY, MADE BY EITHER THE SELLER OR THE BROKER[S].
(If none, state "none," if any listed, indicate by whom the warranty or representation was made). _____

22. BUYER'S RELEASE OF SELLER AND BROKER[S]. The BUYER hereby releases the SELLER and the Broker[s] from any and all liability of any nature relating to the condition of, or any defects in, the premises or any materials, substances or structures or improvements thereon, specifically including, without limitation, all matters set forth in paragraph 21 above, of which the SELLER or Broker[s], as the case may be, had no actual knowledge prior to the execution of this Agreement.

3

Figure 10.3   Purchase and Sale Agreement (Continued)

23. PRESENTATION OF OFFERS. SELLER agrees that upon signing of this Agreement by SELLER and BUYER, and during the pendency of this Agreement, the SELLER's Broker shall have no obligation to present further offers to the SELLER nor shall the SELLER'S Broker continue to market the premises.

24. CONSTRUCTION OF AGREEMENT. This Agreement has been executed in one or more counterparts and each executed copy shall be deemed to be an original, is to be construed under the laws of Massachusetts, is to take effect as a sealed instrument, sets forth the entire agreement between the parties, is binding upon and inures to the benefit of the parties hereto and their respective heirs, devisees, executors, administrators, successors and assigns and may be canceled, modified or amended only by a written instrument executed by the parties hereto or their legal representatives.   If two or more persons are named herein as SELLER or BUYER, their obligations hereunder shall be joint and several.

25. NOTICE. Any notice required to be given in this Agreement shall be in writing and shall be deemed to be duly given when delivered to the party entitled to such notice at their address set forth herein.

26. AGREEMENT TO MEDIATE DISPUTES OR CLAIMS. Any dispute or claim arising out of or relating to this Agreement, the breach of this Agreement or the brokerage services provided in relation to this Agreement shall be submitted to mediation in accordance with the Rules and Procedures of the Homesellers/Homebuyers Dispute Resolution System ("DRS"). Disputes and claims shall specifically include, without limitation, representations made by the SELLER, the BUYER or the Broker[s], in connection with the sale, purchase, finance, condition or other aspect of the premises to which this Agreement pertains, including, without limitation, allegations of concealment, misrepresentation, negligence and/or fraud. Any agreement resolving the dispute or claim signed by the parties pursuant to the mediation conference shall be binding.

The filing of a court action by any party hereto for the purpose of preserving the benefits of this Agreement during the mediation process shall not constitute a waiver or breach of such party's duty to mediate under this paragraph.

By signing this Agreement, the parties hereto acknowledge that they have received, read and understand the DRS brochure and agree to submit disputes or claims as described above to mediation in accordance with the DRS Rules and Procedures. The provisions of this paragraph shall survive the closing of the transactions set forth in this Agreement.

27. ADDITIONAL PROVISIONS. Set forth below are additional provisions, if any, which are incorporated herein and made a part hereof:

(if none, state "none") _____

28. ADDENDUM(S) TO AGREEMENT. Attached hereto is/are addendum(s) which is/are incorporated herein and made a part hereof:

(If none, state "none") _____

SELLER	Date	BUYER	Date
SELLER	Date	BUYER	Date
SELLER'S Broker		Broker	

I have informed the above-named BUYER[S] that I am a:

☐ SELLER'S Agent   ☐ BUYER'S Agent   ☐ Disclosed DUAL Agent

Figure 10.4 Purchase and Sale Agreement

From the Office of:

**STANDARD FORM
PURCHASE AND SALE AGREEMENT**

This _____ day of _____ 19_____

1. PARTIES
    AND MAILING
    ADDRESSES

    (fill in)

    hereinafter called the SELLER, agrees to SELL and

    hereinafter called the BUYER or PURCHASER, agrees to BUY, upon the terms hereinafter set forth, the following described premises:

2. DESCRIPTION
    *(fill in and include
    title reference)*

3. BUILDINGS,
    STRUCTURES,
    IMPROVEMENTS,
    FIXTURES

    (fill in or delete)

    Included in the sale as a part of said premises are the buildings, structures, and improvements now thereon, and the fixtures belonging to the SELLER and used in connection therewith including, if any, all wall-to-wall carpeting, drapery rods, automatic garage door openers, venetian blinds, window shades, screens, screen doors, storm windows and doors, awnings, shutters, furnaces, heaters, heating equipment, stoves, ranges, oil and gas burners and fixtures appurtenant thereto, hot water heaters, plumbing and bathroom fixtures, garbage disposers, electric and other lighting fixtures, mantels, outside television antennas, fences, gates, trees, shrubs, plants, and, ONLY IF BUILT IN, refrigerators, air conditioning equipment, ventilators, dishwashers, washing machines and dryers; and

    but excluding

4. TITLE DEED
    (fill in)
    * Include here by specific
    reference any restric-
    tions, easements, rights
    and obligations in party
    walls not included in (b),
    leases, municipal and
    other liens, other encum-
    brances, and make pro
    vision to protect
    SELLER against BUYER's
    breach of SELLER's
    covenants in leases,
    where necessary

    Said premises are to be conveyed by a good and sufficient quitclaim deed running to the BUYER, or to the nominee designated by the BUYER by written notice to the SELLER at least seven   days before the deed is to be delivered as herein provided, and said deed shall convey a good and clear record and marketable title thereto, free from encumbrances, except

    (a) Provisions of existing building and zoning laws;
    (b) Existing rights and obligations in party walls which are not the subject of written agreement;
    (c) Such taxes for the then current year as are not due and payable on the date of the delivery of such deed;
    (d) Any liens for municipal betterments assessed after the date of this agreement;
    (e) Easements, restrictions and reservations of record, if any, so long as the same do not prohibit or materially interfere with the current use of said premises;
    *(f)

5. PLANS

    If said deed refers to a plan necessary to be recorded therewith the SELLER shall deliver such plan with the deed in form adequate for recording or registration.

6. REGISTERED
    TITLE

    In addition to the foregoing, if the title to said premises is registered, said deed shall be in form sufficient to entitle the BUYER to a Certificate of Title of said premises, and the SELLER shall deliver with said deed all instruments, if any, necessary to enable the BUYER to obtain such Certificate of Title.

7   PURCHASE PRICE
    *(fill in); space is
    allowed to write
    out the amounts
    if desired*

    The agreed purchase price for said premises is

                                                            dollars, of which

    $ have been paid as a deposit this day and
    $
    $ are to be paid at the time of delivery of the deed in cash, or by certified, cashier's, treasurer's or bank check(s).

    $ _____
    $ TOTAL

Source: This form has been made available through the courtesy of the Greater Boston Real Estate Board, and is protected by the copyright laws.

Figure 10.4   Purchase and Sale Agreement (Continued)

8. **TIME FOR PERFORMANCE: DELIVERY OF DEED** *(fill in)*

Such deed is to be delivered at _____ o'clock ___ M. on the _____ day of _____ 19___ at the _____ Registry of Deeds, unless otherwise agreed upon in writing. It is agreed that time is of the essence of this agreement.

9. **POSSESSION AND CONDITION OF PREMISE.** *(attach a list of exceptions, if any)*

Full possession of said premises free of all tenants and occupants, except as herein provided, is to be delivered at the time of the delivery of the deed, said premises to be then (a) in the same condition as they now are, reasonable use and wear thereof excepted, and (b) not in violation of said building and zoning laws, and (c) in compliance with provisions of any instrument referred to in clause 4 hereof. The BUYER shall be entitled personally to inspect said premises prior to the delivery of the deed in order to determine whether the condition thereof complies with the terms of this clause.

10. **EXTENSION TO PERFECT TITLE OR MAKE PREMISES CONFORM** *(Change period of time if desired).*

If the SELLER shall be unable to give title or to make conveyance, or to deliver possession of the premises, all as herein stipulated, or if at the time of the delivery of the deed the premises do not conform with the provisions hereof, then any payments made under this agreement shall be forthwith refunded and all other obligations of the parties hereto shall cease and this agreement shall be void without recourse to the parties hereto, unless the SELLER elects to use reasonable efforts to remove any defects in title, or to deliver possession as provided herein, or to make the said premises conform to the provisions hereof, as the case may be, in which event the SELLER shall give written notice thereof to the BUYER at or before the time for performance hereunder, and thereupon the time for performance hereof shall be extended for a period of thirty _____ days.

11. **FAILURE TO PERFECT TITLE OR MAKE PREMISES CONFORM, etc.**

If at the expiration of the extended time the SELLER shall have failed so to remove any defects in title, deliver possession, or make the premises conform, as the case may be, all as herein agreed, or if at any time during the period of this agreement or any extension thereof, the holder of a mortgage on said premises shall refuse to permit the insurance proceeds, if any, to be used for such purposes, then any payments made under this agreement shall be forthwith refunded and all other obligations of the parties hereto shall cease and this agreement shall be void without recourse to the parties hereto.

12. **BUYER's ELECTION TO ACCEPT TITLE**

The BUYER shall have the election, at either the original or any extended time for performance, to accept such title as the SELLER can deliver to the said premises in their then condition and to pay therefore the purchase price without deduction, in which case the SELLER shall convey such title, except that in the event of such conveyance in accord with the provisions of this clause, if the said premises shall have been damaged by fire or casualty insured against, then the SELLER shall, unless the SELLER has previously restored the premises to their former condition, either

(a) pay over or assign to the BUYER, on delivery of the deed, all amounts recovered or recoverable on account of such insurance, less any amounts reasonably expended by the SELLER for any partial restoration, or

(b) if a holder of a mortgage on said premises shall not permit the insurance proceeds or a part thereof to be used to restore the said premises to their former condition or to be so paid over or assigned, give to the BUYER a credit against the purchase price, on delivery of the deed, equal to said amounts so recovered or recoverable and retained by the holder of the said mortgage less any amounts reasonably expended by the SELLER for any partial restoration.

13. **ACCEPTANCE OF DEED**

The acceptance of a deed by the BUYER or his nominee as the case may be, shall be deemed to be a full performance and discharge of every agreement and obligation herein contained or expressed, except such as are, by the terms hereof, to be performed after the delivery of said deed.

14. **USE OF MONEY TO CLEAR TITLE**

To enable the SELLER to make conveyance as herein provided, the SELLER may, at the time of delivery of the deed, use the purchase money or any portion thereof to clear the title of any or all encumbrances or interests, provided that all instruments so procured are recorded simultaneously with the delivery of said deed.

15. **INSURANCE** *Insert amount (list additional types of insurance and amounts as agreed)*

Until the delivery of the deed, the SELLER shall maintain insurance on said premises as follows:

Type of Insurance	Amount of Coverage
(a) Fire and Extended Coverage	*$
(b)	

16. **ADJUSTMENTS** *(list operating expenses, if any, or attach schedule)*

Collected rents, mortgage interest, water and sewer use charges, operating expenses (if any) according to the schedule attached hereto or set forth below, and taxes for the then current fiscal year, shall be apportioned and fuel value shall be adjusted, as of the day of performance of this agreement and the net amount thereof shall be added to or deducted from, as the case may be, the purchase price payable by the BUYER at the time of delivery of the deed. Uncollected rents for the current rental period shall be apportioned if and when collected by either party.

Figure 10.4   Purchase and Sale Agreement (Continued)

17.	ADJUSTMENT OF UNASSESSED AND ABATED TAXES	If the amount of said taxes is not known at the time of the delivery of the deed, they shall be apportioned on the basis of the taxes assessed for the preceding fiscal year, with a reapportionment as soon as the new tax rate and valuation can be ascertained; and, if the taxes which are to be apportioned shall thereafter be reduced by abatement, the amount of such abatement, less the reasonable cost of obtaining the same, shall be apportioned between the parties, provided that neither party shall be obligated to institute or prosecute proceedings for an abatement unless herein otherwise agreed.
18.	BROKER's FEE *(fill in fee with dollar amount or percentage; also name of Brokerage firm(s))*	A Broker's fee for professional services of is due from the SELLER to the Broker(s) herein, but if the SELLER pursuant to the terms of clause 21 hereof retains the deposits made hereunder by the BUYER, said Broker(s) shall be entitled to receive from the SELLER an amount equal to one-half the amount so retained or an amount equal to the Broker's fee for professional services according to this contract, whichever is the lesser.
19.	BROKER(S) WARRANTY *(fill in name)*	The Broker(s) named herein warrant(s) that the Broker(s) is(are) duly licensed as such by the Commonwealth of Massachusetts.
20.	DEPOSIT *(fill in name)*	All deposits made hereunder shall be held in escrow by as escrow agent subject to the terms of this agreement and shall be duly accounted for at the time for performance of this agreement. In the event of any disagreement between the parties, the escrow agent may retain all deposits made under this agreement pending instructions mutually given by the SELLER and the BUYER.
21.	BUYER's DEFAULT; DAMAGES	If the BUYER shall fail to fulfill the BUYER's agreements herein, all deposits made hereunder by the BUYER shall be retained by the SELLER as liquidated damages unless within thirty days after the time for performance of this agreement or any extension hereof, the SELLER otherwise notifies the BUYER in writing.
22.	RELEASE BY HUSBAND OR WIFE	The SELLER's spouse hereby agrees to join in said deed and to release and convey all statutory and other rights and interests in said premises.
23.	BROKER AS PARTY	The Broker(s) named herein join(s) in this agreement and become(s) a party hereto, insofar as any provisions of this agreement expressly apply to the Broker(s), and to any amendments or modifications of such provisions to which the Broker(s) agree(s) in writing.
24.	LIABILITY OF TRUSTEE, SHAREHOLDER, BENEFICIARY, etc.	If the SELLER or BUYER executes this agreement in a representative or fiduciary capacity, only the principal or the estate represented shall be bound, and neither the SELLER or BUYER so executing, nor any shareholder or beneficiary of any trust, shall be personally liable for any obligation, express or implied, hereunder.
25.	WARRANTIES AND REPRESENTATIONS *(fill in); if none, state "none"; if any listed, indicate by whom each warranty or representation was made*	The BUYER acknowledges that the BUYER has not been influenced to enter into this transaction nor has he relied upon any warranties or representations not set forth or incorporated in this agreement or previously made in writing, except for the following additional warranties and representations, if any, made by either the SELLER or the Broker(s):
26.	MORTGAGE CONTINGENCY CLAUSE *(omit if not provided for in Offer to Purchase)*	In order to help finance the acquisition of said premises, the BUYER shall apply for a conventional bank or other institutional mortgage loan of $ _____ at prevailing rates, terms and conditions. If despite the BUYER's diligent efforts a commitment for such loan cannot be obtained on or before _____, 19____ the BUYER may terminate this agreement by written notice to the SELLER and/or the Broker(s), as agent(s) for the SELLER, prior to the expiration of such time, whereupon any payments made under this agreement shall be forthwith refunded and all other obligations of the parties hereto shall cease and this agreement shall be void without recourse to the parties hereto. In no event will the BUYER be deemed to have used diligent efforts to obtain such commitment unless the BUYER submits a complete mortgage loan application conforming to the foregoing provisions on or before_____ 19_____

Figure 10.4   Purchase and Sale Agreement (Continued)

27. CONSTRUCTION OF AGREEMENT

This instrument, executed in multiple counterparts, is to be construed as a Massachusetts contract, is to take effect as a sealed instrument, sets forth the entire contract between the parties, is binding upon and enures to the benefit of the parties hereto and their respective heirs, devisees, executors, administrators, successors and assigns, and may be cancelled, modified or amended only by a written instrument executed by both the SELLER and the BUYER. If two or more persons are named herein as BUYER their obligations hereunder shall be joint and several. The captions and marginal notes are used only as a matter of convenience and are not to be considered a part of this agreement or to be used in determining the intent of the parties to it.

28. LEAD PAINT LAW

The parties acknowledge that, under Massachusetts law, whenever a child or children under six years of age resides in any residential premises in which any paint, plaster or other accessible material contains dangerous levels of lead, the owner of said premises must remove or cover said paint, plaster or other material so as to make it inaccessible to children under six years of age.

29. SMOKE DETECTORS

The SELLER shall, at the time of the delivery of the deed, deliver a certificate from the fire department of the city or town in which said premises are located stating that said premises have been equipped with approved smoke detectors in conformity with applicable law.

30. ADDITIONAL PROVISIONS

The initialed riders, if any, attached hereto, are incorporated herein by reference.

FOR RESIDENTIAL PROPERTY CONSTRUCTED PRIOR TO 1978, BUYER MUST ALSO HAVE SIGNED
LEAD PAINT "PROPERTY TRANSFER NOTIFICATION CERTIFICATION"

NOTICE: This is a legal document that creates binding obligations. If not understood, consult an attorney.

_____   _____
SELLER (or spouse)   SELLER

_____   _____
BUYER   BUYER

_____
Broker(s)

EXTENSION OF TIME FOR PERFORMANCE   Date _____

The time for the performance of the foregoing agreement is extended until _____ o'clock _____ M. on the _____ day of _____ 19_____ time still being of the essence of this agreement as extended. In all other respects, this agreement is hereby ratified and confirmed.
This extension, executed in multiple counterparts, is intended to take effect as a sealed instrument.

_____   _____
SELLER (or spouse)   SELLER

_____   _____
BUYER   BUYER

_____
Broker(s)

Questions

1. For a contract for the sale of real estate to be valid, the contract must be:

   a. in writing.
   b. signed by the buyer.
   c. signed by the seller.
   d. on a pre-printed standard form.

2. The age of legal competence in Massachusetts is:

   a. 18.   c. 20.
   b. 19.   d. 21.

3. The memorandum required by the Statute of Frauds includes all the following *EXCEPT:*

   a. description of the premises.
   b. identity of the parties and their signatures.
   c. consideration
   d. closing date.

4. *R* makes an offer on *H*'s house. As soon as both parties have signed the contract, *R* is:

   a. immune from the Statute of Frauds.
   b. required to deposit *H*'s earnest money in an escrow account.
   c. the legal owner of the property.
   d. the equitable owner of the property.

5. When an earnest money deposit is received, a broker:

   a. must give it to the seller.
   b. may deposit it in his checking account.
   c. must deposit it in an escrow account.
   d. must hold the check until the closing.

6. When the contract is signed, the buyer becomes the equitable owner. The buyer now has:

   a. legal ownership of the property.
   b. a partnership with the seller.
   c. a deed to the property.
   d. a right to become the owner.

7. A liquidated damages clause permits:

   a. the buyer to recover the earnest money deposit.
   b. the seller to retain all or part of the earnest money deposit.
   c. the broker to retain the earnest money deposit.
   d. the seller to impose a penalty on the buyer in case of a breach.

8. Broker *B* received a buyer's earnest money check for $5,000 and immediately cashed it. At closing, *B* handed the seller a personal check drawn on *B*'s own bank account for $5,300, representing the original earnest money plus 6 percent interest. Which of the following statements is true?

   a. *B* should have deposited the money in a special non-interest-bearing bank account.
   b. *B* properly cashed the check, but should have kept the interest.
   c. *B* should have deposited the money in his personal bank account, and would have been entitled to keep the interest as a service fee.
   d. *B* should have deposited the money in a special bank account, and should have discussed the interest with the parties.

9. *M* and *O* made an offer on a house. The offer was accepted by the seller. The preprinted sales contract used by the broker contained a standard liquidated damages clause. Two weeks later, *M* and *O* decided that they did not want the house. Which of the following statements is true?

   a. They are bound by the sales contract they made and must proceed with the transaction.
   b. The seller and broker may keep the earnest money deposit and put the house back on the market.
   c. The seller may sue both *M* and *O* for breach of contract.
   d. Because the broker used a preprinted form contract, the liquidated damages clause is legally void.

10. Which of the following is seldom used in Massachusetts?

    a. Purchase and sale agreements
    b. Standard pre-printed form contracts
    c. Installment land contracts
    d. Statutory memorandum of sale

11

Transfer of Title

VOLUNTARY ALIENATION

Requirements for a Valid Deed

These are the basic requirements for a valid transfer of real property in Massachusetts:

1. The transfer must be evidenced by a *written document*.

2. The grantor must use the *same full name* as the one by which he or she received title by the previous conveyance. If the name has changed, both the old and new names should be indicated in the document.

3. The grantor must use language that is equivalent to the verb "grant," because that is the purpose of the document.

4. The purchase price or amount of full consideration must be *clearly and completely stated* or the document will not be recordable. Phrases such as "for one dollar and other good and valuable consideration" are not sufficient.

5. The *name of the grantee* and some means of identifying who he or she is and where he or she comes from must be included. If there is more than one grantee, it should be made clear how they are to hold the property.

6. An *accurate description* of the property must be given (see Chapter 8).

7. *Homestead rights* must be released.

8. Acknowledgment must be made before a notary public. A document cannot be recorded in Massachusetts unless it has been *notarized* in order to establish (1) the identity of the maker and (2) that it was signed voluntarily.

9. *Delivery* must be made to the grantee.

10. *Recording* is mandatory in the case of registered land and optional in the case of nonregistered land. (See Chapter 12 of this *Supplement*.)

Types of Deeds

Massachusetts law provides for two forms of deeds for use by individual owners for transfers of property during their lifetimes (*inter vivos* transfers): the *warranty deed* and the *quitclaim deed*.

The Warranty Deed

When the statutory short form *warranty deed* is used, the grantor warrants that:

- he or she held the premises in *fee simple*;

- the granted premises were *free from all encumbrances not specifically stated*;

- he or she had *good right to sell and convey*; and

- he or she *warrants and defends the title against the lawful claims and demands of all persons*.

The Quitclaim Deed

In a *quitclaim deed* the grantor warrants that *at the time of delivering the deed*:

1. the premises were *free of all encumbrances made by the grantor*; and

2. the grantor will warrant and defend the title for the grantee against the lawful claims of all persons *claiming by, through or under him or her but against no one else.*

(Note that this is different from the definition given in the main text.)

The acceptance of a deed generally ends a buyer's right to claim that the title is faulty. For this reason, a title search is recommended.

Contract terms that extend to issues beyond the deed — warranties or promises about the condition of the property that were part of a purchase and sale agreement, for instance — may survive beyond acceptance of a deed. Such terms may form the basis for a later lawsuit.

Transfer Tax Stamps

In Massachusetts, the tax levied on the conveyance of real estate is $2.28 for each $500 (or fraction of $500) of real estate equity transferred from buyer to seller. The tax is paid by the seller, who must purchase *revenue stamps* (also called *excise* or *conveyance tax stamps*) at the Registry of Deeds and affix them to the deed before recording. Stamps are not required on other real estate documents, such as mortgages or leases.

MATH CONCEPT...
Calculating Massachusetts Transfer Taxes

I.

Bob purchases Sandy's home for $175,000 in cash.

There are 350 "taxable units" in 175,000:

$175,000 ÷ 500 = 350$

Sandy's transfer tax is 350 × $2.28 = $798.

II.

Steve buys Bills's home for $195,000, by taking over Bill's existing $100,000 mortgage and paying $95,000 in cash. Bill pays the tax only on the *equity* transferred. His equity of $95,000 is the price of $195,000 less the $100,000 mortgage, which he does not pay off at the sale but transfers with the property.

There are 190 "taxable units" in $95,000:

$95,000 ÷ 500 = 190$

Bill's transfer tax is 190 × $2.28 = $433.20.

III.

Sarah buys Carol's home for $175,100.

There are 351 "taxable units" in 175,100:

$175,100 ÷ 500 = 350.2 = 351$ (the .2 is a fraction of 500, and so counts as a full 500)

Carol's transfer tax is 351 × $2.28 = $800.28

Compare this result with example I.

INVOLUNTARY ALIENATION

The period in Massachusetts for which a person must use a parcel of real estate to establish ownership by *adverse possession* is 20 years. The requirements are the same as for the easement by prescription described in Chapter 6 of this *Supplement*.

The requirements are:

• continuous or uninterrupted use or possession;

• without the permission of the owner;

• for 20 years; and

• with the actual or constructive knowledge of the owner.

Title acquired by this means is subject to legal technicalities and should not be relied on without legal advice. Adverse possession may *not* be maintained against any state-owned land or registered land (see Chapter 12 of this *Supplement*).

TRANSFER OF A DECEASED PERSON'S PROPERTY

Transfer of Title by Will

In Massachusetts, any person 18 years of age or older may make a will. In addition to the requirements set out in the text, a valid will must be attested by two witnesses. The witnesses do not have a right to read the will, but they must be aware that the testator is signing a document he or she knows to be his or her will. The witnesses should see the testator sign the will and should see each other sign as witnesses. Any devise or legacy given to a witness is void.

A surviving spouse has a *right of election*, and may have the will's provisions for the spouse set aside. The spouse can claim his or her dower or curtesy rights, or may take property under the law of intestate distribution. (Dower and curtesy, and the spousal homestead right, are discussed in Chapter 6 of this *Supplement*.)

Transfer of Title by Descent

When a person dies without leaving a valid will, his or her property passes by *intestate succession* under the terms of Massachusetts law. After payment of all debts, claims and taxes, the estate is divided according to statute, depending on the status of the decedent. The chart in Figure 11.1 shows the most common statutory distributions.

Figure 11.1   Statutory Distributions

DECEDENT STATUS	FAMILY STATUS	HOW PROPERTY PASSES
Married with surviving spouse[1]	No children No other relatives	100% to surviving spouse
	Children[2]	50% to surviving spouse 50% shared by children or descendants of deceased child
Married no surviving spouse	Children	Children share equally, with descendants of a deceased child taking their parent's share
Unmarried no children	Relatives	100% to father or mother, brothers or sisters, or other relatives
	No relatives	100% to Massachusetts by escheat

[1]Massachusetts law allows the decedent's spouse the right to elect a life estate of dower or curtesy, as discussed in Chapter 6 of this *Supplement*, in place of the share provided for in the law of descent.

[2]Adopted and biological children are treated equally.

Questions

1. The law of descent and distribution applies when a person dies:

   a. testate.
   b. leaving no heirs.
   c. leaving minor children.
   d. intestate.

2. Jim was a witness to his Uncle John's will. When the will was read after John's death, Jim discovered that he was a devisee of his uncle's will. Which of the following statements is true?

   a. Because Jim is a witness, the devise is void.
   b. As a witness, Jim should have read the will.
   c. Because Jim is a witness, the will is void.
   d. Jim has a right of election.

3. How is the voluntary transfer of real estate during a person's lifetime accomplished?

   a. By the right of election
   b. By a will
   c. By a deed
   d. By an antenuptial agreement

4. When title is conveyed using a quitclaim deed, the grantor warrants that at the time of delivery:

   a. the premises are free of all encumbrances made by the grantor.
   b. the premises are free of all encumbrances made by past owners.
   c. he or she will defend the title against the claims of all people.
   d. None of the above

5. For the transfer of title to be valid, which of the following requirements does *not* necessarily apply?

   a. There must be a written document.
   b. Language equivalent to the word "grant" must be used.
   c. The purchase price must be mentioned.
   d. The deed must be recorded at the Registry of Deeds.

6. Which of the following is *not* required to acquire land by adverse possession?

   a. Use with the owner's permission
   b. Use for a period of 20 years
   c. Use openly so as to be seen
   d. Use without the owner's permission

7. The Smarts sold their house to the Youngs for $203,500. The Youngs paid the entire amount out of their cash assets. How much will the revenue stamps cost?

   a. $565.48   c. $927.96
   b. $900.00   d. $945.56

8. The Browns sold their house to the Greens for $150,800. The Browns had $40,000 left on their assumable mortgage, which the Greens assumed. How much will the revenue stamps cost?

   a. $505.25   c. $344.28
   b. $50.16   d. $506.16

9. Which of the following is *not* included in a statutory short form warranty deed?

   a. The grantor held the property in fee simple.
   b. The premises are free of encumbrances.
   c. Title is warranted only against claims of persons by, through or under the grantor.
   d. The grantor has good right to sell and convey the property.

10. For a deed to be valid, it must be acknowledged and delivered to the:

    a. grantor.
    b. Registry of Deeds.
    c. grantee.
    d. notary public.

11. One of the purposes of the notary's acknowledgment is to:

    a. give constructive notice.
    b. show the deed was signed voluntarily.
    c. show the deed is valid.
    d. protect the grantee.

12. *L* accepts a statutory short-form quitclaim deed from *M*. Later, a claim against the property is made by *N*, who has a valid outstanding lien against *O*, who owned the property before *M*. Which of the following best states what can happen under these circumstances?

    a. *L* can force *M* to pay the claim.
    b. *M* cannot be held under his quitclaim covenants.
    c. *L* can force *O* to pay the claim.
    d. No claim can be made because *L* has a valid deed.

13. Harold thought wills were unlucky, so he never had one made. Last week, Harold was struck by a meteor and died. He is survived by his wife, Wanda, and two adult children, Sam and Debbie. How is Harold's estate divided?

    a. All of Harold's estate passes to Wanda.
    b. One third to Wanda, and one third each to Sam and Debbie.
    c. One half to Wanda, one quarter each to Sam and Debbie.
    d. $200,000 to Wanda, and on half of the remaining estate to Sam and Debbie.

14. Same facts as in 14, only this time Sam and Debbie are also struck by the meteor and die at the same time as Harold. Sam has one child, George. Debbie has two children, Glen and Glenda. How is Harold's estate divided?

    a. One quarter each to Wanda, George, Glen and Glenda.
    b. One half to Wanda, and the remaining half divided equally among George, Glen and Glenda.
    c. All of Harold's estate passes to Wanda.
    d. One half to Wanda, one quarter to George and one eighth each to Glen and Glenda.

15. The decedent, Donna, left an estate valued at $800,000 after the payment of all taxes and debts. She had no surviving husband, but three children: Alan, Brenda and Charles. Alan, who died shortly after his mother, has two children, one of whom is adopted. Brenda has three children and Charles has two. Alice did not write a will. How is her property divided?

    a. Brenda and Charles each take $400,000.
    b. Brenda and Charles each take $266,666, and Alan's children each take $133,333.
    c. Brenda takes $342,857.13, Charles takes $228,571.42, and each of Alan's children take $114,285.71.
    d. The estate will escheat to Massachusetts.

16. Doug and Darryl both die, leaving estates of well over $1 million each. Neither wrote a will. Doug's parents live in Argentina and haven't spoken to him since 1975. Darryl, who has no family members, left a note in a sealed envelope stating his wish that his property be given to a local animal shelter. How will their estates be divided?

    a. Both will escheat to Massachusetts.
    b. Doug's estate will go to his parents, and Darryl's will go to the shelter.
    c. Doug's estate will escheat to Massachusetts, and Darryl's will go to the shelter.
    d. Doug's estate will go to his parents, and Darryl's will escheat to the state.

12

Title Records

PUBLIC RECORDS

Recording

The recording system is a semi-voluntary system in Massachusetts. A grantee is not required to record a document under the Massachusetts recording statute, although he or she may choose to do so. The law clearly places the risk that results from not recording on the person who chooses not to record. A conveyance must be recorded to be effectively executed.

There are, however, several ways in which a purchaser can get notice. Possession of the property, for example, may serve as notice just as effectively as recording the deed.

Deeds, conveyances, leases and mortgages are recorded with the Registry of Deeds of the county in which the real estate is situated. Recording establishes the order of priority of an interest or lien.

Registered Land

There are two kinds of real property in Massachusetts:

1. *registered land*, and

2. land that is not registered.

"Registered" is not the same as "recorded." Any grantee may record his or her deed, giving notice to the world that he or she is the new owner. However, property that has been registered must be re-registered every time it is transferred or subdivided.

System of Registration

The system of land registration used in Massachusetts is similar to the Torrens system described in the main text.

Registration is commenced with an action to "quiet title," in which the court is asked to determine who actually owns a parcel of land and what claims or liens against the property are valid. An exhaustive investigation of the history of the property's ownership is conducted. Advertising and any other possible means of reaching anyone who may have a claim on the property are used. Usually, the property will be surveyed, and its boundaries firmly established.

The court then holds a hearing at which all persons have a right to present their claims. At the conclusion of this action, the court will order the property to be registered and a numbered certificate will be issued to the rightful owner. The certificate, called a *land court certificate*, will show the legal description, the owners and their interests, as well as the valid claims and liens that the court has determined to be outstanding against the property. From that day onward, the land is registered, and a special set of rules and laws governs the title to it.

Any time registered land is conveyed, the deed must be accompanied by the land court certificate, and must be presented to the land court for reregistration in the name of the new owner. *The transfer is not valid until the land is reregistered.* Similarly, attempts to encumber registered land are invalid until the encumbrance is registered on the certificate in the land court office.

Normal recording of documents will not affect registered land until registered on the land court certificate. Once land has a *registered title* (also called a *land court title*), registration is mandatory, and forever. The papers and documents filed in a registration action are held, recorded and indexed by a recorder, who is appointed by the governor and under the direction of the chief justice of the land court.

It should be noted that the land court's records office is part of the court, and is not the same as the Registry of Deeds.

EVIDENCE OF TITLE

In Massachusetts, it is the *buyer* who customarily has title searched and the property surveyed. The seller does not have to share in these expenses unless he or she agrees to or unless there is a defect in the title.

Most buyers hire an attorney to make a title search, particularly because banks will not loan money on property that has not had the title searched. The attorney may make one of three types of title search:

- a *title search and opinion*, in which the attorney searches the public records, lists the entries, and states his or her opinion of the title;

- a *full abstract*, in which the attorney copies the important parts of each document that affects the title, and then states his or her opinion; or

- a *certificate of title*, which is simply a brief statement of the attorney's opinion.

Often, however, buyers may forego a title search if the bank with which they will place their mortgage conducts its own. If the title is found to be faulty after the bank lends money to the buyer, the bank can sue the attorney who conducted the search to recover the mortgage amount. Similarly, if the buyer paid the bank for the lawyer's title search, and the property involved is an owner-occupied home

with fewer than four families, then the attorney will be liable to the buyer for the full purchase price. In either case, the attorney will not be liable if he or she was not negligent in conducting the search.

An increasing number of lending institutions in Massachusetts require title insurance as part of the mortgage commitment. There are generally two forms of title insurance available to homeowners: one protects only the lender's interest, while the other (more expensive) form protects the interests of both. Title insurance is discussed in Chapter 12 of the main text.

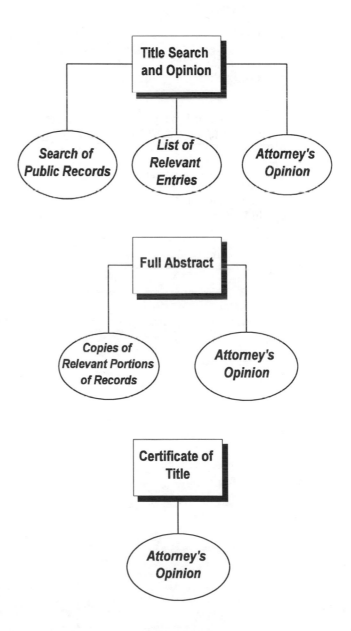

Questions

1. Mr. Hawkins buys real estate that is registered land. For the transfer to be valid he must:

   a. record the deed at the Registry of Deeds.
   b. reregister the land in his name.
   c. institute a suit to quiet title.
   d. record the land court certificate in his name.

2. In Massachusetts, who customarily pays for the title search?

   a. The bank
   b. The buyer
   c. The seller
   d. The broker

3. Which of the following is *not* a title search method commonly used by an attorney in Massachusetts?

   a. Land court certificate
   b. Title search and opinion
   c. Certificate of title
   d. Full abstract

4. Title insurance provides a means of financial protection if:

   a. the bank had a title search conducted.
   b. the buyer did not pay the lawyer.
   c. a defect is found in the title.
   d. the seller paid for the title search.

5. Deeds, conveyances, leases and mortgages are usually recorded:

   a. with the land court recorder.
   b. in order to establish a deed's validity and to prove that delivery occurred.
   c. with the Registry of Deeds of the county in which the land is located.
   d. with the Registry of Deeds of the county in which the seller resides.

Real Estate License Laws

WHO MUST BE LICENSED

In Massachusetts, anyone who acts as "real estate broker" or "real estate salesperson" (see Chapter 4) must be licensed. In an action to recover consideration owed for real estate brokerage services (that is, a commission), the person seeking to recover must prove that he or she was duly licensed at the time the services were performed. Any person who acts as a broker or salesperson without a license is subject to a find of up to $500.

Exceptions

The Massachusetts Real Estate License Law does not apply to:

- persons selling, buying, exchanging, renting or leasing their own property;

- managing agents or regular employees of managing agents who perform any real estate activities as part of their regular duties;

- licensed auctioneers;

- persons who deal in securities or certificates of beneficial interests in trusts;

- public officers or employees who are performing their official duties;

- persons who are acting as attorney-in-fact under authority of a power of attorney from an owner that authorizes them to complete a real estate transaction;

- attorneys (unless they are performing the duties of a broker for a commission, in which case they must pay a fee to be licensed, but do not have to take a licensing examination);

- receivers, trustees, administrators, executors or other persons appointed by or acting under a court order;

- trustees or their regular employees acting under written instruments of trust, deeds or declarations of trust, or wills; and

- banks, credit unions and insurance companies acting as fiduciaries, negotiating a mortgage on real estate or acting for themselves.

BOARD OF REGISTRATION OF REAL ESTATE BROKERS AND SALESMEN

The Massachusetts Board of Registration of Real Estate Brokers and Salesmen (referred to in this chapter as "the board") administers the license laws. The board consists of five members appointed by the governor to five-year terms. Three members must be full-time licensed real estate brokers who have been active in the real estate business for at least seven years. The other two members are designated representatives of the public. Members serve without compensation, but are reimbursed for expenses incurred in carrying out their duties.

The board must hold at least four regular meetings each year. Written records must be kept of all meetings, and must be open to the public for inspection. The board must submit an annual report to the governor that details its proceedings and expenses.

LICENSING PROCEDURE

Anyone who performs real estate brokerage services, as either a broker or salesperson, must be licensed. No salesperson may conduct or operate his or her own real estate business, or act in any way except as the representative of a real estate broker.

Requirements for Issuance of License

As you already know, anyone who wants to be a real estate broker or salesperson must take and pass a written examination.

Every applicant for a salesperson's license must submit proof that he or she has completed 24 classroom hours of instruction in real estate subjects. An applicant for a broker's license must prove that he or she has been actively associated as a salesperson with a real estate broker for at least one year, and has completed a total of 30 additional classroom hours of instruction. A broker's license may not be issued to anyone younger than 18.

(A nonresident may be licensed as a broker and as a salesperson in Massachusetts if he or she is licensed in another state. A licensed nonresident is not required to take the broker's or salesperson's exam, or to maintain an office in Massachusetts.)

Each applicant must furnish evidence of good moral character. If a corporation, society, association or partnership applies for a broker's license, evidence of the good moral character of all the officers and directors, or holders of similar positions, or of all the partners, must also be furnished.

All applications must be accompanied by the recommendations of three reputable citizens who reside in Massachusetts and are not related to the applicant. The recommendations must state that the applicant has a good reputation for honesty and fair dealing.

An applicant may be required to appear for a personal interview with the board.

The board may also require an applicant to submit a report from an independent source regarding the applicant's previous occupation, or other material information.

Issuance of a Broker's License to Corporations and Other Entities

A broker's license may be held by a corporation, society, association or partnership. At least one officer or partner must be designated as the entity's representative for the purpose of obtaining a license. Each designated officer or partner must apply to the board for a broker's license in his or her own name.

A salesperson's license, however, may not be issued to a corporation, society, association or partnership.

Examination

The broker's or salesperson's licensing examination is prepared by ASI, the board's designated independent testing service. The examination is designed to enable the board to determine the competence of the applicant to transact the business of a real estate broker or salesperson in Massachusetts.

There is no limit on the number of applicants who may take the examination on any examination date. The broker's examination must be offered at least six times a year, and the salesperson's examination at least eight times a year.

To enter the examination, the examinee must have two forms of identification, one of which must be a picture identification, such as a driver's license.

The following rules apply to the examination process:

- Examinees may not refer to any notes, books or memoranda.

- All computations must be shown on blank pages provided for that purpose. Calculators may be used only if they are hand-held, battery-operated and nonprogrammable, without a tape output.

- The copying of questions or the making of notes about questions is prohibited.

- No one may remove copies of the examination from the examination room either before or after the examination.

- Examinees may not leave the examination room for any reason until they have turned in the complete examination to the proctor.

- An applicant who fails to attain a passing score may file an application for reexamination.

Violation of any rule may result in the disqualification of an applicant.

Issuance of License

A real estate license is valid for a period of two years. It may be renewed biennially, provided that the application for renewal is not made later than one year from the expiration date of the license. The license originally issued to an individual is valid until the licensee's next birth date occurring more than 24 months after the original date of issuance.

The fees for issuance and renewal of a broker's or salesperson's license are waived for blind persons and paraplegic veterans.

An applicant for a broker's license must provide the board with a $1,000 bond, payable to the Commonwealth, for the benefit of any person injured by the broker's actions.

In the event that a licensed broker who is the sole proprietor of a real estate business should die, the board may issue a temporary license.

The temporary license authorizes a licensee to continue the operation of the business for up to one year from the broker's date of death.

Usual Place of Business

A licensed resident broker must maintain a usual place of business within Massachusetts, and must conspicuously display his or her license (or a certified copy). The broker must notify the board of any change of business location. Failure to notify the board is grounds for revoking the broker's license.

Suspension, Revocation or Refusal of Renewal of License

In the event that the board receives a verified, written complaint about a broker or salesperson, his or her license may be suspended, revoked or not renewed if the board finds that the broker or salesperson:

- obtained his or her license by false or fraudulent representation;

- knowingly made any substantial misrepresentation;

- acted in the dual capacity of broker and undisclosed principal in the same transaction;

- acted for more than one party to a transaction without the knowledge and consent of all the parties;

- failed to account for or remit any money belonging to others that has come into his or her possession as a broker or salesperson;

- paid commissions or fees to an unlicensed person who acted as a real estate broker or salesperson, and who was required to have been licensed;

- accepted, gave or charged any undisclosed commission, rebate or profit on expenditures for a principal;

- induced any party to break a real estate contract or lease for the personal gain of the licensee;

- commingled the money or other property of a principal with his or her own;

- failed to give both the buyer and the seller a copy of the purchase and sale agreement;

- committed any act expressly prohibited by the Real Estate License Law;

- affirmatively solicited residential property for sale, lease or listing on the grounds of alleged change of value due to the presence or the prospective entry into the neighborhood of a person or persons of another race, economic level, religion or ethnic origin, or distributed material or made statements designed to induce a residential property owner to sell or lease in response to such a change in the neighborhood. A violator is also subject to a fine of from $1,000 to $2,500 and/or up to six months in prison (see Chapter 21);

- engaged in the sale of real property located in a land development in another state, promoted or advertised in Massachusetts, the owner or developer of which failed to comply with all filing requirements; or

- accepted a net listing from a prospective seller.

The board may also suspend, revoke or refuse to renew the license of a person who has been convicted of a criminal offense in Massachusetts or any other state, if the offense demonstrates his or her lack of good moral character to act as a real estate broker or salesperson.

If a licensed salesperson or broker is found to have committed unlawful discriminatory practices in violation of Chapter 151B, his or her license will be suspended for 60 days. If the violation has occurred within two years of a prior violation, the license will be suspended for 90 days (see Chapter 21).

Any suspension, revocation or refusal to renew may be reconsidered by the board.

The suspension or revocation of a broker's or salesperson's license does not free them from liability for any other penalties or punishments provided by law.

Enforcement

The board is empowered to conduct investigations and hearings, and to take other appropriate and necessary action to enforce the license law. All complaints submitted to the board must be in writing and signed by the complainant.

The board may summon witnesses and demand the production of books and papers. Testimony may be taken by deposition as in a civil action, and any member of the board may administer oaths, examine witnesses and receive evidence.

In the event that a witness fails or refuses to appear and testify, the superior court has jurisdiction to issue an order compelling the witness to appear.

Decisions of the board must be by majority, expressed in writing, and signed by all the members. Copies must be sent to each interested party.

The board's decision may be appealed to the superior court within 20 days following notification of the decision.

Broker/Salesperson Relationship

A licensed salesperson must be engaged by a licensed broker. That is, *a licensed salesperson may not conduct his or her own real estate business*. A broker may not be licensed as a salesperson while retaining his or her broker's license; similarly, a salesperson may not be both a salesperson and a broker at the same time.

Brokers must furnish the board with the names, addresses and license numbers of all brokers and salespersons engaged by them. The board must also be notified of all terminations of the broker-salesperson relationship.

A broker who is employed by another broker may not engage any real estate salesperson.

Advertising

"Blind" advertising is prohibited. Any advertisement placed by a broker must affirmatively and unmistakably state that the advertiser is a real estate broker and not a private party. However, if the broker is the actual owner of the property being sold, this requirement does not apply.

Advertisements may not be limited to post office box numbers, telephone numbers or a street address: the broker's business name and address must appear in the advertisement.

Salespersons are prohibited from independently advertising. As with all other activities, the advertising of property must be under the direct supervision of a broker, and in the broker's name. Of course, if the salesperson is advertising his or her own property, he or she has all the rights of any owner.

Brokers may not advertise in a manner that indicates, either directly or indirectly, any unlawful discrimination against any individual or group on the basis of race, creed, color or national origin (see Chapter 21).

The licensing law forbids discrimination based on race, creed, color or national origin, but many other state and federal laws add the following classifications, which also may be bases for illegal discrimination in housing: sex or sexual preference; physical or mental handicap; marital or family status; presence of a child or children; AIDS or HIV infection; age; veteran status; or receipt of public or rental assistance (see Chapter 21).

Handling Others' Money

One of the most common grounds for discipline of licensees in Massachusetts is the failure to properly handle and account for money.

Unless otherwise agreed to in writing by the parties, all money received by the broker that belongs to another party must be deposited in a fiduciary bank account maintained by the broker as a depository for funds. The account may be interest-bearing, but the interest must be included in the proper accounting at the end of each transaction, and the parties must agree to the earning and distribution of interest.

All deposits or payments received by a real estate salesperson, or by a broker engaged by another broker, must be turned over to the engaging broker.

Every broker must keep records of funds deposited in his or her escrow account. All such funds and records are subject to inspection by the board or its agents.

Disclosure of Interest in Property

A real estate broker or salesperson may not, either directly or indirectly, buy property in which he or she has acquired an interest, or which he or she has listed without first fully disclosing his or her interest. The owner must acknowledge that disclosure has been made.

Before a real estate broker or salesperson buys property for a client in which he or she, or any relative, has an interest, the interest must be disclosed to all parties. Similarly, a real estate broker or salesperson must disclose to a purchaser any interest he or she or any relative may have in any property prior to its sale.

A broker may not take an option to purchase property for which he or she has been approached to act as a broker without first disclosing that he or she is now acting as a prospective buyer rather than as a broker or agent for the owner.

Use of Attorney

No broker or salesperson may advise against the use of an attorney's services in any real estate transaction.

Duty to Report All Offers

All offers obtained by brokers or salespersons on a property must be immediately presented to the owner. It is the owner's right to decide whether an offer is legitimate or unreasonable.

Agency Disclosure

All real estate brokers or salespersons must provide each prospective purchaser and seller with a notice disclosing the broker's or salesperson's relationship with the prospective purchaser or seller (see Chapter 4). The notice must be provided at the time of the *first personal meeting* between the broker or salesperson and the seller or purchaser where a *specific property* is discussed, where the broker or salesperson represents either the seller or the purchaser *exclusively*.

Dual agency is permitted if both parties give their informed written consent.

Written notice of an agency relationship does not have to be given individually to each prospective purchaser who attends an open house. Agency disclosure in that situation may be made by other means, such as a poster, flyer or property description form.

APARTMENT LISTING SERVICES

No one other than a licensed real estate broker or salesperson may engage in the business of finding rental housing for prospective tenants for a fee. The Real Estate License Law regulates how apartment listing services may be provided.

A listing may not be provided to a customer unless the service has verified the apartment's availability within eight days prior to offering the listing. The listing must include:

- the apartment's address, availability date, monthly rent and utility costs;

- the number of rooms and bedrooms;

- whether or not the apartment is to be shared, and whether or not pets are permitted;

- whether or not elevator service is available, and the apartment's vertical floor location; and

- the date the apartment's availability was last verified, and the name, address and telephone number of the person to contact for rental.

During the period of the contract between a customer and the service, the customer must be sent a listing of all available apartments that meet the customer's requirements. The listing must be sent at least twice a week.

In the event a customer has not rented an apartment at the expiration of the contract with the apartment rental service, the service is required to refund all money paid by the customer in excess of $30. The customer must request the refund in writing, and the refund must be paid within 15 days of receiving the request.

An apartment listing service may not advertise an apartment as available without authorization from the landlord, or without verifying the apartment's availability within the 24-hour period preceding the publication deadline for the advertisement.

In addition, a service may not:

- advertise or represent that it has listings that meet certain specifications if it does not in fact have such listings, or advertise apartments that do not actually exist;

- fail to disclose that it is a listing service and not a landlord or owner;

- fail to cancel advertisements for apartments that are no longer available within 24 hours; or

- induce a customer to sign a contract by falsely representing that the service has listings that conform to the customer's requirements.

If a specific category of apartments is advertised (rather than simply the service itself), the following disclosure must be included in the ad:

"NOTICE: WE ONLY PROVIDE LISTINGS OF APARTMENTS AND HAVE NO CONTROL OVER THE ACTUAL RENTAL OF ANY APARTMENTS."

PROMOTIONAL SALES OF OUT-OF-STATE PROPERTY

The promotional sale of out-of-state property is strictly regulated by the real estate license law. No real property located outside Massachusetts may be offered for sale or sold in the Commonwealth unless it is offered for sale and sold through a real estate broker licensed in Massachusetts. "Real property" includes land, buildings, fixtures, condominiums, cooperatives and time-sharing intervals.

An out-of-state development property may not be offered for sale until the owner or developer has applied to the board for investigation of the property. The developer must provide the board with an extensive array of documentation, statements and data regarding the property, including information on how deposits will be handled, a description of the development's topography and soil, sample advertisements, a financial statement and a price list covering specific plots to be sold and the terms and conditions of sale offered to prospective buyers. The developers are responsible for bearing the cost of an on-site inspection by the board.

Questions

1. The Board of Registration of Real Estate Brokers and Salesmen was created to:

   a. make new laws.
   b. make recommendations to the legislature.
   c. administer the license laws.
   d. raise money for the state.

2. Applicants for a salesperson's license must:

   a. be at least 18 years old and have completed a 12-hour exam prep course.
   b. have completed 24 classroom hours of instruction in real estate subjects.
   c. have been actively engaged in real estate activities for at least six months.
   d. submit recommendations from three persons, two of whom are Massachusetts residents.

3. Which of these is *not* exempt from the license law?

   a. A salesperson employed by a broker
   b. A receiver acting under a court order
   c. A loan officer in a credit union
   d. A licensed auctioneer

4. In the event of the death of a sole proprietor, a temporary license is issued. The license:

   a. is good for one year and is not renewable.
   b. may be renewed if necessary.
   c. becomes a permanent license after one year.
   d. is given automatically.

5. A corporation may have a broker license if:

   a. all its officers are personally licensed as real estate brokers.
   b. one officer is licensed as a broker and designated to perform all real estate duties.
   c. the corporation applies for a license.
   d. the corporation already has a salesperson's license.

6. Lenny holds a Massachusetts real estate broker's license. His brother took (and passed) the Massachusetts exam for Lenny, because Lenny's car wouldn't start that day. Lenny lives in Massachusetts, but his only office is in Borderton, New Hampshire, which is only five minutes from the Massachusetts border. In his office, Lenny keeps his license locked safely in a file cabinet in the basement. Lenny recently sold a house to the Feldspars, although he neglected to mention to them that he was the owner of the house. Lenny deposited the Feldspars' earnest money in his wife's checking account for safe keeping. After closing the sale, Lenny visited neighboring homeowners to give them his card and to mention that the Feldspars were poor immigrants from Iceland who practiced a strange Viking religion, whose presence in the neighborhood would be likely to depress everyone else's property values. *How many violations of the Massachusetts license law has Lenny committed?*

   a. 2   c. 6
   b. 4   d. 0: his office is in N.H.

7. Which of the following, if true, would *not* be grounds for revoking the broker's or salesperson's license?

   a. Paying a commission to an unlicensed person who acted as a real estate salesperson
   b. Inducing a seller to break a contract so the broker can present a higher offer
   c. Affirmatively soliciting residential properties for sale
   d. Accepting a disclosed, voluntary net listing from a prospective seller

8. When a complaint has been filed with the board against a licensee,

   a. the licensee must cease acting as a salesperson.
   b. the licensee's license is immediately revoked.
   c. the accused is tried in superior court.
   d. the board holds a hearing.

9. All deposits or payments of money received by a broker or salesperson must be:

   a. kept in a designated location in the broker's office.
   b. placed in the salesperson's savings account.
   c. deposited in a special bank account maintained by the broker for such deposits.
   d. immediately turned over to the seller.

10. A licensed salesperson may advertise:

   a. property personally listed by him or her.
   b. property he or she owns.
   c. property only after getting the owner's permission.
   d. any listed property, provided the ad is not discriminatory.

11. When a licensed broker changes his or her place of business,

   a. a new license will be issued by the board immediately.
   b. his or her license may be revoked if the board is not notified.
   c. a new license will be issued for a full term.
   d. the new address must be approved by the board.

12. If a customer of an apartment rental service has not rented an apartment by the time the contract expires, any payment made by the customer is excess of $30 must be refunded within:

   a. 24 hours.   c. 15 days.
   b. 10 days.   d. 30 days.

13. An apartment rental service may *not*:

   a. take exclusive listings.
   b. advertise a property without the owner's permission.
   c. retain copies of signed contracts for more than 18 months.
   d. advertise an existing vacant apartment.

14. Broker Edna has received three offers on a property within an hour. The property is listed for $210,000. Offer A is for $209,500; Offer B is for $190,000; Offer C is for $175,000. What should she do?

   a. Ignore Offer C because it is ridiculously low.
   b. Find out if the makers of Offers A and B want to raise their offers under the circumstances.
   c. Present all offers immediately.
   d. Present the highest offer only.

15. The Board of Registration is informed that a broker was guilty of discrimination on June 20 of this year. The broker had been found guilty of a similar charge on June 5 of the previous year. The board will suspend the broker's license for how many days?

   a. 50   c. 45
   b. 60   d. 90

Figure 13.1   Fees

(Fees charged by the licensing board change periodically. You may enter the current fees in the blanks below.)

ACTIVITY	WHEN PAYABLE	AMOUNT
Examination Fee	At time of application	
Broker's License		$_____
Salesperson's License		$_____
Issuance of License	On notice of passing exam	
Broker's License		$_____
Salesperson's License		$_____
Issued to Corporation		$_____
Renewal Fee	Every two years	
Broker's License		$_____
Salesperson's License		$_____
Issued to Corporation		$_____
Promotional Sale of Out-of-State Property	At time of filing	$_____

Real Estate Financing: Principles and Practice

MORTGAGE LAW

Massachusetts is a *title theory* state. That means that the mortgage "splits" title to the property — the mortgagee takes legal title, while equitable title is retained by the mortgagor.

The granting of the property to the mortgagee by the mortgagor is done with an instrument that is similar to a warranty deed, except that the document contains provisions permitting the mortgagor to get the property back if he or she fulfills certain conditions. Generally, these conditions are:

- Pay back the sum of money with interest as provided in a separate promissory note

- Keep the property insured for the benefit of the mortgagee

- Promptly pay the taxes assessed against the property

- Keep the property in good repair (do not allow the property to be "wasted")

- Do not remove any buildings or improvements from the property.

FINANCING TECHNIQUES

Massachusetts banks are permitted to make, purchase, participate in or service a wide variety of statutorily approved real estate mortgage loans, including certain loans in excess of 95 percent of value; open-end mortgages; and reverse mortgage loans.

AMORTIZED LOANS

In Massachusetts, amortized mortgage loans are referred to as *direct reduction loans*.

DEFAULT

Default occurs when any condition of the mortgage is not satisfied by the mortgagor. The mortgagee will make use of an *acceleration clause*, which causes the entire debt to be due immediately. In most Massachusetts mortgages, the mortgagee will have included a power of sale giving it the right to immediately possess the property, to advertise the property as having been foreclosed and, after a stated period, to sell the property and apply the proceeds to the unpaid balance of the loan.

The advertising period for a foreclosure is once a week for three weeks prior to the foreclosure, with the announcements appearing in a general-circulation newspaper published in the county in which the property is located.

If the mortgage does not include a power of sale clause, the mortgagee must institute specific proceedings prior to selling the property. In either case, any proceeds obtained from the sale of the property in excess of the amount of the loan, interest and court costs belong to the mortgagor.

A defaulting borrower may cure all defaults before the foreclosure sale. The borrower may also refinance the loan with another lender to pay off the defaulted mortgage debt or to obtain sufficient funds to bid for the property at the foreclosure sale. No redemption is allowed after a mortgage foreclosure sale is complete.

Questions

1. Massachusetts is a(n):

    a. lien theory state.
    b. intermediate theory state.
    c. title theory state.
    d. warranty deed state.

2. The granting of property to a mortgagee by the mortgagor is accomplished through a document similar to a:

    a. quitclaim deed.
    b. warranty deed.
    c. defeasance clause.
    d. title registration.

3. In Massachusetts, an amortized mortgage loan is referred to as a:

    a. straight loan.
    b. traditional mortgage.
    c. direct reduction mortgage.
    d. direct reduction loan.

4. The usual period during which Massachusetts lenders advertise a property as having been foreclosed prior to sale is how many weeks?

    a. 1   c. 3
    b. 2   d. 4

5. A foreclosure on property must be advertised in a(n):

    a. official foreclosure newsletter distributed in the mortgagee's county of residence.
    b. newspaper published in the mortgagee's county of residence.
    c. newspaper published in the county in which the property is located.
    d. official publication circulated in the county in which the property is located.

6. How long is the defaulted borrower's redemption period after a foreclosure sale is complete?

    a. One year
    b. Six months
    c. Three years
    d. There is no redemption period.

7. After a mortgage foreclosure sale, the money in excess of the loan, interest and court costs belongs to the:

    a. devisee.
    b. mortgagee.
    c. grantor.
    d. mortgagor.

8. The provision in a mortgage that permits the mortgagee to demand the full amount of the loan in the event the borrower defaults is called a(n):

    a. direct reduction clause.
    b. redemption clause.
    c. immediate possession clause.
    d. acceleration clause.

16

Leases

LEASING REAL ESTATE

In Massachusetts, leases for more than one year must be in writing to satisfy the statute of frauds. Leases for seven years or more must be written, acknowledged and recorded or their validity will be restricted to the original landlord.

Breach of Lease

If a tenant fails to pay the rent on time, a landlord can begin a statutory eviction proceeding. Massachusetts law provides specific procedures that must be followed to evict a tenant. For instance, a landlord cannot simply seize the property as soon as the rent payment deadline passes. The landlord must give two weeks' written notice to the tenant, who may prevent eviction by paying all overdue rent, plus the landlord's expenses, at any time during the two-week period.

In a tenancy at will, the law requires that the landlord give the tenant as much time to stay in the property as one rental period after the landlord provides a notice to quit the property. The minimum period of notice is 30 days (seven in the case of rooming houses in which rent is due weekly), and the maximum is three months. Generally, the notice is effective at the beginning of the next rental period. A landlord may include in the notice an offer to allow the tenant to stay under terms different from the existing agreement.

STANDARD LEASE PROVISIONS

Certain lease provisions are legally void and unenforceable in Massachusetts. A lessor may not include a provision in the lease permitting him or her to enter the premises for any reason other than to make repairs or to show it to a prospective lessee. A lease may not require the tenant to waive the landlord's responsibility to keep the premises habitable, or to waive the landlord's liability for failing to provide heat, light, power or other utilities or services required by the lease.

No lease may contain a provision permitting the landlord to terminate it in the event the tenant should have children.

A landlord may not interfere with a tenant's right of *quiet enjoyment* of the premises — that is, the right to uninterrupted use of the property during the term of the lease. Prohibited interference includes failing to repair or maintain the premises, as well as active interference, such as efforts to regain possession of the property. A landlord who interferes with a tenant's right of quiet enjoyment may be subject to a fine and imprisonment, as well as damages of up to three months' rent.

FOR EXAMPLE ...

The smoke detectors in Larry Landlord's property malfunctioned and sounded loud alarms for three days, until the batteries finally died. The tenant sued, and Larry was held liable for three months' rent.

Tenants in Lucy Lessor's building were without hot water for three weeks. The tenants were not entitled to three months' rent, however, since Lucy had immediately hired a work crew to correct the problem as quickly as possible.

The landlord may enter the property without violating the tenant's right of quiet enjoyment:

- to make necessary repairs;

- to show the property to a prospective tenant; or

- if it appears that the tenant has abandoned the property, or if the tenant has given notice that he or she is leaving and is within the last 30 days of the rental so that a damage inspection is appropriate.

Security Deposit

A lessor may require a prospective tenant to pay a security deposit prior to the beginning of the lease term. However, at the time the lease commences, no tenant may be required to pay an amount in excess of

- the first month's rent; plus

- the last month's rent; plus

- a security deposit equal to the first month's rent; plus

- the purchase and installation cost of a new key and lock.

If a security deposit is required, the landlord must provide the tenant with a separate written statement of the property's condition at the time it is leased. Both the tenant and the landlord (or the landlord's agent) must sign the statement.

The security deposit does not belong to the landlord. It remains the tenant's property, and the landlord must deposit it in a separate bank account within Massachusetts. It may not be commingled with the landlord's own assets. The tenant is entitled to the return of the security deposit within thirty days of the termination date of the lease. The landlord must pay interest on the security deposit and last month's rent at the prevailing annual interest rate, if the money has been kept for more than one year.

The landlord is entitled to withhold three deductions from the security deposit:

1. any unpaid rent;

2. any unpaid increase in real estate taxes for which the tenant is liable under the lease; and

3. the reasonable cost of repairing damage caused by the tenant, excluding normal wear and tear.

If the cost of repairing damage is withheld from the security deposit, the landlord has 30 days in which to provide the tenant with a detailed, itemized list of the damages and repair costs, supported by such evidence as bills or receipts.

In the event that the lessor transfers the property, the account containing the tenant's security deposit is also transferred to the new owner. If the lessor fails to transfer the account, the tenant is entitled to stay on in the premises past the termination date of the lease for a period equivalent to the rental value of the security deposit.

The landlord forfeits his or her right to retain any part of the security deposit if he or she:

- fails to deposit the funds in an independent interest-bearing account;

- fails to furnish the tenant with an itemized list of damages;

- fails to transfer the deposit to a new owner;

- includes and attempts to enforce an invalid provision in the lease, such as one waiving the tenant's rights; or

- fails to return the balance of the security deposit to the tenant within thirty days of the termination of the lease.

Pro-Tenant Legislation

The rights and obligations of landlords and tenants in Massachusetts are regulated under the Massachusetts Consumer Protection Act, discussed in Chapter 4.

In addition to those already discussed, some of the prohibited actions include:

- renting property that contains a condition dangerous to the health, safety or well-being of the occupants, or failing to repair such conditions;

- failing to keep promises made to the tenant at the time of renting;

- failing to reimburse the tenant for repairs the tenant made after being authorized by the landlord;

- failing to comply with state or local housing codes;

- demanding an increase in rent to pay higher taxes on the property unless a written lease obligates the tenant to do so;

- failing to make the written rental agreement clear and simple;

- depriving the tenant access to his or her dwelling without a proper court order or beginning court proceedings without following the statutory time limits; and

- imposing interest on any payment until it is more than 30 days overdue.

A tenant is entitled to enforce his or her rights, either through legal action or by informing an appropriate authority of the landlord's failure to comply either with the terms of the lease or with housing laws or building codes. Landlords are prohibited from retaliating, or threatening retribution, against the tenant.

Fair Housing

Discrimination in renting or leasing is prohibited under Massachusetts law, and is discussed in detail in Chapter 21 of this *Supplement*.

Questions

1. A 14-month lease would have to be:

    a. written, acknowledged and recorded.
    b. written and recorded.
    c. written.
    d. recorded.

2. If a lease runs for seven years or longer, it must be:

    a. written, acknowledged and recorded.
    b. written and recorded.
    c. written.
    d. recorded.

3. A landlord who wants to begin statutory eviction proceedings *cannot*:

    a. seize the property for nonpayment of rent.
    b. bring a writ in the court for eviction.
    c. bring a separate writ for the unpaid rent.
    d. give the tenant notice to quit the property.

4. John and Sally are tenants at will. Their rent is due the first of the month. The landlord has given them a notice to quit the property the day before the rent is due. How many days do they have before they must vacate the property?

    a. 14   c. 10
    b. 30   d. 90

5. A tenant's right of quiet enjoyment is the right to:

    a. be free from noise.
    b. uninterrupted use of the premises.
    c. limited use of the premises.
    d. remain on the premises after breaching the lease.

6. The violation of the right of quiet enjoyment may result in:

    a. immediate eviction.
    b. imprisonment, but no civil damages.
    c. imprisonment, a fine, and damages of up to three months' rent.
    d. eviction after 30 days' notice.

7. The landlord may not ask for:

    a. the last month's rent.
    b. a lock and key deposit.
    c. two month's security deposit.
    d. one month's security deposit.

8. The security deposit must be kept:

    a. in a Massachusetts bank account.
    b. in the landlord's possession.
    c. in the landlord's bank account.
    d. in a trust fund established for the tenant.

9. The owner of rented space is called the:

    a. lessor.   c. REALTOR®.
    b. vendor.   d. mortgagee.

10. After the lease terminates, the tenant is entitled to the return of his or her security deposit:

    a. within 30 days, including interest.
    b. within three weeks, including interest.
    c. unless the property has been transferred to a new owner.
    d. with no deductions withheld.

11. The rights and obligations of landlords and tenants are regulated by the:

    a. Massachusetts Tenant's Rights Act.
    b. Massachusetts Antidiscrimination Act.
    c. Massachusetts Consumer Protection Act.
    d. Massachusetts Landlord/Tenant Act.

12. Which of the following is *not* a prohibited landlord action?

    a. Renting dangerous property
    b. Failing to comply with housing codes
    c. Failing to reimburse a tenant for authorized repairs
    d. Requiring an amount equal to 3 months' rent at the time the lease commences.

Real Estate Appraisal

APPRAISING

Regulation of Appraisal Activities

In Massachusetts, real estate appraisal is a regulated profession, like real estate.

Appraisers are required to be certified or licensed by the state to appraise property for compensation in all but nonfederally related transactions. The licensing or certification requirement for appraisers does not, however, prevent a real estate broker or salesperson from giving his or her *opinion* of a property's value in the ordinary course of business, as long as he or she does not refer to the opinion as an "appraisal."

There are four classes of real estate appraisers recognized in Massachusetts:

1. State-certified general real estate appraiser

2. State-certified residential real estate appraiser

3. State-licensed real estate appraiser

4. Real estate appraisal trainee.

To be a state-certified appraiser, an individual must meet the requirements of the Appraisal Foundation's Appraisal Qualifications Board and pass a state-administered examination. An appraiser may be state-licensed if he or she meets the requirements of the Federal Financial Institutions Examination Council or its Federal Appraisal Subcommittee and passes a state-administered exam. No examination is required for trainees.

State-certified appraisers may appraise all types of real property, while state-certified residential real estate appraisers and state-licensed appraisers are limited to the appraisal of certain residential property. Certified appraisers must meet the qualification standards of the Appraisal Foundation, while licensed appraisers must meet the minimum requirements of Title XI (see Chapter 18 in the main text). Trainees' activities are limited to assisting certified and licensed appraisers in the performance of appraisal assignments.

To be licensed or certified, an appraiser must demonstrate (on a written examination) several areas of expertise. A licensed or certified appraiser must demonstrate knowledge of the technical terminology of real estate appraisal, appraisal report writing and real estate economics. He or she must have an understanding of the principles of land economics and real estate appraisal processes, as well as the challenges of gathering, interpreting and processing data.

An appraiser must have an understanding of the standards for developing and communicating appraisals, and a basic comprehension of the theories of depreciation, cost estimating, methods of capitalization and appraisal mathematics.

Finally, an appraiser must have a basic understanding of real estate law, and must be aware of the types of misconduct for which disciplinary proceedings may be instituted.

The following acts or omissions are some of those may form the basis for revoking or suspending an appraiser's license or certificate:

- procuring or attempting to procure a certificate or license by providing false or incomplete information;

- procuring or attempting to procure a certificate or license by means of bribery, misrepresentation, or fraud;

- conviction of a crime substantially related to real estate appraisal;

- entry of a civil judgment against the appraiser based on an allegation of fraud, misrepresentation or deceit;

- conviction of any felony;

- any act or omission involving dishonesty, fraud or misrepresentation with the intent to either benefit the appraiser or injure another person;

- violating the confidentiality of government records; and

- negligence, incompetence, or failure to exercise reasonable diligence in developing an appraisal, preparing an appraisal report, or communicating an appraisal.

An appraiser may not accept any appraisal assignment contingent on the appraiser reporting a predetermined estimate, analysis or opinion, or where the fee is contingent on the appraiser reporting a particular valuation.

A certificate or license is renewable every three years from its first date of issuance, provided that the appraiser complies with continuing education requirements. An appraisal trainee may renew his or her trainee license only once.

Questions

1. Real estate appraisers must comply with state licensing regulations:

   a. unless they are licensed real estate brokers.

   b. unless the transaction is not federally related.

   c. unless they have already taken a written examination.

   d. unless the property's value has been previously agreed upon.

2. The four categories of real estate appraisers recognized in Massachusetts are:

   a. certified general; certified residential; licensed; trainee.

   b. licensed general; licensed residential; licensed trainee; certified.

   c. qualified general; Appraisal Foundation licensed; Federal Appraisal certified; trainee.

   d. pre-license appraiser; pre-certification appraiser; appraiser; appraiser-trainee.

3. Real estate brokers and salespersons:

   a. may not estimate a property's value unless they are certified or licensed appraisers.

   b. may appraise a property if they disclose that are not professional appraisers.

   c. may offer a seller an "Appraisal Opinion" of the value of the seller's property.

   d. may offer their opinion of the value of a property, but may not call it an appraisal.

4. A state-certified appraiser:

   a. may appraise only residential property.

   b. may appraise any real property.

   c. may only assist a state-licensed appraiser.

   d. may list and sell real estate for a commission.

5. The real estate appraiser examination:

   a. must be taken every three years.

   b. includes real estate law.

   c. must be taken only by candidates for licensed residential real estate appraiser.

   d. includes depreciation and capitalization, but not economics.

6. Laverne is a licensed real estate appraiser. She is convicted of fraudulently reporting a low appraised value on certain property so that the loan would be denied and her friend Shirley could step in and buy the property for less money. She is also convicted of robbing a bank.

   Laverne's license:

   a. will not be revoked if she takes and passes the licensing examination.

   b. will be revoked because of the fraud conviction, but not because of the robbery.

   c. will be revoked because of both the fraud and robbery convictions.

   d. will not be revoked: Shirley did not personally benefit from the fraud, and bank robbery is not substantially related to appraisal.

Land Use and Development

PUBLIC LAND-USE CONTROLS

Zoning Regulations

Through power conferred by state enabling acts, each city and town in Massachusetts develops its own city plan and zoning ordinances or bylaws. The Zoning Enabling Act, Chapter 40A of the Massachusetts General Laws, is the source of zoning authority for all communities in the state except Boston. It sets forth procedural rules for establishing zoning ordinances.

The enabling act specifically exempts land and buildings that did not conform to the prescribed use for the location at the time the zoning code was passed. The statute indicates that *nonconforming uses* may not continue forever and prescribes that if the use is abandoned, the current zoning code must be followed.

Application for a Variance

Objections to the zoning of particular pieces of land may be taken to the zoning board of appeals. Applicants for zoning variations must demonstrate that the desired variance will be in the public interest and that it will remain within the spirit of the ordinance. The applicant also must show that the change is necessary because of the hardship caused by the existing requirement and that the variance would affect only his or her property and not the general district. Decisions of the zoning board of appeals may be appealed to the Massachusetts superior court.

Zoning regulations do not affect the marketability of title to real estate. However, buyers should protect themselves in purchase agreements by including a contingency clause for securing the necessary permits and approvals from local zoning authorities before the buyers take title.

Planning Boards

In addition to local zoning boards, Massachusetts law provides for the creation of local and regional planning boards in all parts of the state. Planning boards have two major functions: planning and subdivision control. Subdivision control consumes most of a board's time, especially in growing suburban and rural areas.

Subdivision Control. Subdivisions are defined in Massachusetts as land divided into two or more lots that do not front on a public or approved road. The basic purposes of subdivision control include:

- protecting the health, safety, convenience and welfare of inhabitants;

- providing adequate access by roads that are safe and convenient for travel;

- lessening congestion on subdivision roads and adjacent public roads;

- reducing motor vehicle accidents;

- securing safety in case of fire, flood, panic and other emergencies; and

- securing adequate provision for water, sewer, drainage and underground utility services.

To fulfill these objectives, planning boards must ensure not only that subdivision plans conform to local zoning bylaws, but also that developers provide adequately designed and constructed streets, installation of necessary utilities and installation of drainage facilities.

To ensure compliance, planning boards may draft rules and regulations requiring environmental impact statements, compliance with board of health restrictions, strict and well-defined road and drainage standards and specifications and performance bonds to ensure completion of roads and drainage systems.

When a subdivision plan is submitted, the board must give public notice and hold a public hearing. In addition, county officials may require a subdivision survey and plot plan to be recorded with each subdivision contingent on the local planning board's approval of the plan.

Uniform Building Code. The Uniform Building Code regulates residential, commercial and industrial construction in Massachusetts. It supersedes local building codes.

"Anti-Snob" Zoning. In response to selective zoning practices in many cities and towns in the Commonwealth, the Massachusetts legislature enacted an "anti-snob" zoning law in 1969. The law allows certain public agencies and any nonprofit or limited divided organization to construct low-income and moderate-income housing despite local zoning bylaws. The local board of appeals conducts a public hearing to determine whether an applicant qualifies for a "comprehensive permit" to begin construction, which eliminates the need for the applicant to file more than once.

The law also provides criteria to determine whether a city or town has met the regional need for low-income or moderate-income housing. If the need has not been met, the local board of appeals has a statutory duty to override the local bylaws, codes and regulations.

PRIVATE LAND-USE CONTROL FOR SUBDIVISIONS

Subdividers usually place restrictions on the use of subdivision lots to benefit all lot owners. To be valid, a parcel of adjacent land must benefit from the restriction. A subdivider may establish restrictions through a covenant in a deed or by a separate recorded declaration.

Much of the old common law governing restrictions has been changed by state statutes. In Massachusetts, restrictions may be created to exist for any length of time, but unless the creating document includes a definite time limit, they become void after 30 years.

Courts will refuse to enforce a restriction if:

* changes in the neighborhood have frustrated the purpose of the restriction;

* the parties who have the right to enforce the restriction have acted in such a way as to make enforcement unfair;

* the general plan first contemplated by the subdivider has been abandoned or no longer exists;

* the highest and best use of the land is impeded by the restriction; or

* enforcement of the restriction is inequitable.

Persons who seek to have the restriction removed must demonstrate that the restriction is unenforceable for one or more of these reasons.

Environmental Protection Legislation

Control of environmental issues at the state level is exercised by the Department of Environmental Management. Environmental regulations are addressed in the Appendix to this *Supplement*.

Questions

1. Zoning ordinances are developed by:

   a. the Zoning Enabling Act.
   b. each city and town.
   c. each county.
   d. the local building inspector.

2. The Smiths' store does not conform to the current zoning ordinances, passed after they'd been in business for several years. After the store is destroyed by fire, the Smiths want to go back into business. If the new store will not conform to current zoning, what will they be required to do if they wish to continue their old business?

   a. Rebuild an exact replica of the old store.
   b. Abide by the current zoning ordinances.
   c. Apply for a variance.
   d. Get a permit for a new building.

3. The owners of Blasto Concrete feel that their property has been improperly zoned for residential use. Their objection may be taken directly to the:

   a. Massachusetts Superior Court.
   b. Zoning Board of Appeals.
   c. Department of Environmental Management.
   d. Zoning Enabling Board.

4. Local and regional planning boards have two major functions:

   a. planning and building code enforcement.
   b. planning and "anti-snob" zoning control.
   c. planning and establishing uniform zoning ordinances.
   d. planning and subdivision control.

5. A subdivision is land that does not have frontage on a public or approved road and is divided into how many lots?

   a. 2 or more   c. 5
   b. 50   d. 25 or more

6. Which of the following is *not* a purpose of subdivision control?

   a. Reducing motor vehicle accidents
   b. Ensuring the highest and best use of land
   c. Protecting health, safety, convenience and welfare
   d. Securing safety in case of emergencies

7. Residential, commercial and industrial construction in Massachusetts is regulated by:

   a. the Uniform Building Code
   b. local planning boards
   c. local building codes
   d. local zoning ordinances

8. The purpose of Massachusetts' "anti-snob" law is to:

   a. ensure that local zoning ordinances do not bar low- and moderate-income housing.
   b. secure adequate provision of services to low- and moderate-income residents.
   c. establish construction standards for low- and moderate-income housing.
   d. enforce a uniform zoning law that creates mandatory low- and moderate-income housing projects in higher-income areas.

9. If a subdivider's restriction on the use of subdivision lots does not contain a specific time limit, it will automatically become void after how many years?

   a. 10   c. 30
   b. 25   d. 40

10. Which of the following arguments is *least* likely to persuade a Massachusetts court to refuse to enforce the subdivision restriction?

    a. "The creating document contained no time limit, and was written in 1964."
    b. "The surrounding neighborhood has changed considerably."
    c. "The restriction is not popular with the property owners."
    d. "The restriction interferes with the highest and best use of the land."

Fair Housing Laws and Ethical Practices

MASSACHUSETTS LAWS AGAINST DISCRIMINATION

Both Massachusetts and federal antidiscrimination laws bar discrimination against certain classes of persons. The federal laws are discussed extensively in the text. In Massachusetts, it is illegal to discriminate based on the following considerations:

RACE	SEX
RELIGION	SEXUAL PREFERENCE
AGE	PHYSICAL HANDICAP
ANCESTRY	HIV/AIDS STATUS
VETERAN STATUS	COLOR
NATIONAL ORIGIN	FAMILY STATUS
MENTAL HANDICAP	CHILDREN
RELIANCE ON PUBLIC ASSISTANCE	RELIANCE ON RENTAL ASSISTANCE

While discrimination against persons who have children is prohibited, the prohibition does not apply to any situation in which the state sanitary code regarding the number of persons who may safely occupy the premises would be violated.

The provisions of Massachusetts law regarding fair housing practices regulate the activities of *all persons* who have an ownership interest of any kind in real property: not just to real estate licensees. The broad prohibitions include discrimination:

- in offering residential and commercial property for sale or lease;

- in granting mortgage loans;

- in appraising residential real estate; and

- in offering membership or participation in multiple listing or other brokers' organizations.

Prohibited Activities

Massachusetts' Antidiscrimination laws apply to the following types of real estate:

- Multiple dwellings (three or more independent family units) or continuously located housing accommodations, including publicly assisted housing

- Single-family residences that are directly *or through an agent* offered to the public for sale, lease or rental by advertising in a newspaper or otherwise, by signs and notices located on the premises or elsewhere, by listing with a broker or by other means of public offering

- Commercial space

The following activities are specifically outlawed:

- Refusing to rent, lease, sell or negotiate the sale of any property as a means of discrimination

- Discriminating against any person or group in the terms, conditions or privileges involved with the possession or acquisition of property

- Making any inquiry or record regarding the race, creed, color, national origin, sex, sexual orientation, age, ancestry or marital status of a person seeking to rent, lease or buy property, or concerning the fact that the person is a veteran or a member of the armed forces, or blind

- Making false representations regarding the availability of suitable housing, including failing to show all properties listed for sale or rent that are within the requested price range

Discrimination is illegal if its purpose is to relieve the owner of the responsibility for removing or covering lead paint. Similarly, no real estate agent may refuse to accept a listing from, or otherwise discriminate against, a homeowner whose property contains urea formaldehyde foam insulation (UFFI) and indoor formaldehyde levels below 0.10 parts per million (see the Environmental Appendix to this *Supplement*).

Exceptions

While there are some limited exceptions to the general rules barring discrimination, real estate professionals should regard all discrimination as suspect, and should not rely on a possible exception as a means to commit a discriminatory act. It should be noted that the exceptions under state law may not be permitted under federal Antidiscrimination laws.

In Massachusetts, it is permissible to inquire into an applicant's age for the purpose of determining his or her creditworthiness, as long as no negative weight is given to applicants over age 62. It is also not illegal to refuse a mortgage or other credit to a minor, or to a person whose life expectancy is shorter than the duration of the mortgage.

It is legal for a residential community to designate certain structures as housing for persons over age 55 or 62 on one or more contiguous parcels totaling more than five

acres. State- or federally-assisted housing developments for the elderly are also legal.

As a rule, the term "age discrimination" does not apply to minors. Property owners and managers, landlords, lenders and real estate agents may lawfully discriminate against minors *as clients*. This should be distinguished from discrimination against families with children, which is illegal.

"Sexual orientation" does not include persons whose orientation involves minor children as sex objects.

Two-family owner-occupied residences are exempt from Massachusetts antidiscrimination laws (except with regard to persons receiving public or rental assistance).

While an owner is generally required to bear the reasonable expense of modifying structures to make them accessible to handicapped persons (including those with mobility, hearing or sight impairments), he or she is not required to pay for unreasonable modifications. A modification or accommodation is considered unreasonable if it imposed an undue hardship on the owner, based on such factors as:

- the cost and extent of the modification or accommodation;

- the modification's effect on the property's market value;

- the type and size of the property; and

- the availability of federal tax deductions.

No owner is required to bear the cost of modifying more than 10 percent of the units in his or her property to make them fully accessible to a person using a wheelchair. No additional rent or other charge for handicapped-accessible housing may be imposed, however.

Blockbusting

The practice of **blockbusting** is prohibited both by statute (Chapter 151B) and by the Massachusetts Real Estate Brokers' and Salesmen's License Law (Section 87 AAA). Blockbusting is described in detail in Chapter 21 of the main text.

Steering

Massachusetts law (Chapter 151B) prohibits the practice of **steering**, which is discussed in detail in Chapter 21 of the main text.

Notices

Chapter 151B requires that a notice that states that the agency or office complies with the provisions of Massachusetts laws against discrimination must be conspicuously displayed in every real estate agency and rental office. The display also may include a summary of unlawful activities.

Any real estate agency or rental office that fails to comply with this requirement is subject to a fine of up to $100.

Enforcement

Because many of the provisions of the Massachusetts laws against discrimination are similar to those of the Federal Fair Housing Act of 1968, the Massachusetts regulations have been ruled "substantially equivalent to the federal law." For this reason all fair housing complaints in Massachusetts are referred to and investigated by the Massachusetts Commission Against Discrimination, an agency that reports directly to the governor's office.

Complaints brought under the laws against discrimination must be filed with the commission within six months after the alleged discriminatory actions occur. The commission investigates all complaints and notifies the board of its findings. On finding probable cause for a complaint, the commission sends the accused violator a conciliation agreement ordering him or her to comply with the law, or to make some specific restitution or take other affirmative actions.

The commission may award up to $1,000 in damages to persons against whom the accused has discriminated, and the board may suspend the real estate agent's license. The suspension for a first-time violation is 60 days. A 90-day suspension may be issued if the violation occurs within two years of a prior violation.

Any person who refuses to comply with the commission's orders may appeal to the Massachusetts Superior Court.

Questions

1. Which of the following is *not* included under the Massachusetts fair housing laws?

   a. Veteran's status
   b. Marital status
   c. Bankruptcy status
   d. Public assistance status

2. Barbara Broker has four prospective clients: *J* refuses to sell to Roman Catholics; *K* refuses to sell to people of Welsh descent; *L* refuses to sell to people who own foreign cars; and *M* refuses to sell to "rich white guys." Which of Barbara's prospective clients is engaging in unlawful discrimination?

   a. *J*, *K* and *L* only   c. *J*, *K* and *M* only
   b. *L* and *M* only   d. *J*, *K*, *L* and *M*

3. Mr. Smith is moving to Washington, and has given Broker Bob the listing for renting his house. He gave Bob instructions that the property was not to be shown to people with children. Bob should:

   a. inform the Fair Housing Authority.
   b. inform the Board of Registration.
   c. accept the listing.
   d. refuse the listing.

4. Massachusetts' Antidiscrimination laws *do not* apply to which of the following types of real estate?

   a. Single-family residences sold by the owner
   b. 2-unit owner-occupied residential dwellings
   c. Residential dwellings of 3 or more units
   d. Commercial buildings in commercially-zoned areas.

5. Two people come into Broker Betty's office: *Y* is a blind woman in a wheelchair, and *Z* is a homosexual man. By refusing to show them any properties, Betty has committed unlawful discrimination against:

   a. *Y* only   c. both *Y* and *Z*
   b. *Z* only   d. neither *Y* nor *Z*

6. Broker Ben is offered an expensive listing in a desirable neighborhood. The house contains urea formaldehyde insulation. Ben may:

   a. accept the listing and show the house as he would any other property.
   b. refuse the listing on the grounds that urea formaldehyde insulation is hazardous.
   c. accept the listing, but show the property only to members of certain ethnic groups.
   d. accept the listing, but not actively market the property.

7. Two people applied for 30-year mortgages with Mighty Mortgage Company: *R*, a 14 year-old boy; and *S*, a 98 year-old man. Both were asked their ages. If *R* and *S* are turned down, Mighty Mortgage has unlawfully discriminated against:

   a. neither *R* nor *S*   c. *S* only
   b. *R* only   d. both *R* and *S*

8. Larry Landlord owns a 30-unit apartment building. What is the maximum number of units he can be required to bear the cost of modifying to comply with Massachusetts law regarding the accommodation of a person using a wheelchair?

   a. All ground-level units   c. 5
   b. 3   d. 10

9. All fair housing complaints in Massachusetts are referred to and investigated by the:

   a. Massachusetts Commission Against Discrimination.
   b. governor's office.
   c. federal Fair Housing Commission.
   d. Massachusetts Superior Court.

10. License suspensions for a real estate agent found to have violated the anti-discrimination laws are how many days for: (i) a first violation, and (ii) a second violation within 2 years?

    a. (i) 30 and (ii) 60   c. (i) 60 and (ii) 120
    b. (i) 60 and (ii) 90   d. (i) 90 and (ii) 120

Environmental Issues and the Real Estate Transaction

ENVIRONMENTAL ISSUES

Massachusetts, along with most other states, has recognized the need to balance the legitimate commercial and residential use of land with the necessity of preserving vital resources and ensuring the quality of the air, water and soil. Preservation of the state's natural environment enhances both the quality of life and property values. The prevention and clean-up of pollutants and toxic wastes not only revitalizes the land but creates greater opportunities for responsible development. The main text provides a comprehensive discussion of environmental issues and hazardous substances.

Massachusetts Law

The attorney general of Massachusetts is authorized to prevent or remedy damage to the environment. "Damage to the environment" means the destruction, damage or impairment of any of Massachusetts' natural resources.

The statutory definition includes air and water pollution, improper sewage disposal, use of toxic pesticides, and excessive noise. Improper operation of dumping grounds; impairment of rivers, streams, floodplains, lakes, ponds and other surface or subsurface water resources; and destruction of seashores, dunes, marine resources, underwater archeological resources, wetlands, open spaces, natural areas, parks and historic districts or sites are all addressed by statute.

Hazardous Waste

The Massachusetts Oil and Hazardous Material Release Prevention and Response Act is the state-level implementation of the federal Comprehensive Environmental Response, Compensation and Liability Act (CERCLA). If any toxic chemicals or petroleum products are on or under the soil of property, the information should be given to a prospective buyer. If the owner suspects the presence of any hazardous waste, he or she should have an expert examine the soil. If toxins are present, arrangements will be made for their removal by the proper state authority. This environmental clean-up law is sometimes referred to as "Superfund."

The law provides that the manager, transporter or generator of hazardous wastes is responsible for cleaning up these wastes if they are spilled or improperly disposed of. If the responsible party cannot be found, then the site owner or landowner is held responsible for cleaning up the site. The state will move ahead and do the work, then record a claim (lien) at the Registry of Deeds for the cost. This lien takes priority over all other recorded liens, except when the greater part of the property is used for single-family or multifamily housing, in which case the lien follows other encumbrances. The lien remains on the property until the state files a release.

Generally, property may not be sold or transferred once a hazardous waste has been discovered. If it is necessary for the state to clean up the pollution, a lien will exist against the property for the value of the cleaning costs. Owners may occasionally escape liability if they can establish that they are innocent landowners who took reasonable steps to determine the presence of hazardous waste when they purchased the property in question.

Because an automatic lien against the tainted land takes precedence over mortgages, most banks will demand that the property be inspected before they commit to a loan. The broker will have to negotiate the costs of the inspection between the seller and the buyer.

Figure A.1 illustrates an inspection contingency addendum to an offer, providing for the inspection of property for the presence of oil or hazardous materials.

Wetlands

Land in Massachusetts that is in a wetland or bordering a wetland is legally protected property. Under the Wetlands Restriction Act, the Department of Environmental Protection may draw "non-encroachment lines" around any waterway in order to restrict harmful or destructive activities such as dredging, filling, or polluting. The Coastal Zone Management and Ocean Sanctuaries Acts both restrict the use and development of the state's coastline out to the three-mile territorial limit. The Scenic Rivers Act, the Clean Waters Act and a wide array of air, water and land pollution regulations work together to protect Massachusetts' fragile wetland areas from the side effects of land development.

Scenic Roads

Massachusetts' rural roads are protected by a law enacted in 1973 that recognizes that trees and stone walls that border local roads have scenic, aesthetic and historic

value. Any repair, maintenance, reconstruction or paving work that involves destruction of trees or stone walls within the right-of-way of a rural road may not be undertaken until the planning board has held a public hearing and granted written permission for the work to commence.

HAZARDOUS SUBSTANCES

Lead-Based Paint

The Massachusetts Lead Law requires the removal of lead paint by the owner of a property if children under six years of age live there. The Lead Law and its disclosure requirements apply to residential properties constructed before 1978 that are offered for sale or rental. Adult rooming houses are exempt, as are short-term vacation rental properties leased for fewer than 31 days, unless the lead paint is chipping or peeling.

Lead paint must be removed or covered ("encapsulated") if found on window sills, stair risers, woodwork, doors, interior wall corners, stair risers and railings up to a height of five feet. Any chipped or cracked plaster or paint must be removed. Flat wall surfaces do not normally have to be deleaded. In short, the deleading requirement applies to all "mouth-able" surfaces accessible to a child under the age of six.

Owners or brokers of pre-1978 properties may not discriminate against potential buyers or tenants who have children who would force lead abatement repairs to be done.

While there is no requirement that a lead inspection be undertaken prior to selling or purchasing a home, brokers and owners are required to notify prospective purch-asers if lead paint is present and that licensed inspectors are available who can determine the levels of lead content. Sellers must inform purchasers of actual or possible lead hazards whether or not a real estate broker is involved in the sale.

A state-approved disclosure form *must* be signed by the purchaser, certifying that he or she has been informed of the existence of a lead paint hazard. The disclosure must be accompanied by a property transfer notification, published by the Department of Public Health, which presents information on lead-based paint, childhood lead poisoning, and the legal requirements of the Lead Law in a question-and-answer format. In addition, real estate agents must verbally inform purchasers of the Lead Law's abatement requirement, and of their right to have a lead inspection of the property.

If the purchaser wants to have an inspection performed, the seller must allow at least an additional ten days' time prior to closing. The purchase and sale agreement may or may not be contingent on the property passing the inspection tests. If no test is performed on a pre 1978 property prior to closing, the purchaser has 90 days after closing to have the property inspected. A purchaser is required to abate a lead hazard within 90 days of securing title to the property if a child under six will live in it. A tax credit of up to $1,500 is available to owners to offset the cost of abating or containing lead paint, including the cost of replacing windows. Figure A.2 illustrates a lead paint contingency addendum to an offer.

Urea Formaldehyde Foam Insulation (UFFI)

UFFI was installed as an insulating material in many properties in the late 1970s. Because the presence of airborne formaldehyde in sufficient concentrations presents a serious health hazard, the use of UFFI has been banned in Massachusetts.

The perceived risks of exposure to UFFI can cause a property's value to decrease significantly. Nonetheless, the listing broker should determine whether UFFI was installed, and a written disclosure and signed acknowledgment should be submitted if the material is present. Property owners are obligated by law to take reasonable steps to determine if UFFI is present. "Reasonable steps" means examination of household insulation records for properties purchased before January 1, 1970, and a visual inspection in the case of homes purchased after January 1, 1970. A buyer must be provided with an explanatory "UFFI Information Sheet" published by the Department of Public Health, along with the seller's disclosure of the presence of UFFI. Similarly, landlords of residential dwellings that contain UFFI must provide disclosure statements to all prospective tenants prior to entering into a lease agreement (see Figure A.3).

Both brokers and owners are subject to heavy fines for failing to disclose the presence of UFFI.

Nonetheless, no real estate broker or salesperson may discriminate against a homeowner whose property contains UFFI if the indoor ambient formaldehyde level is below 0.10 parts per million.

Neither air testing nor disclosure is required for home equity or home improvement loans.

"Title 5:" On-Site Sewage Disposal Systems

Few changes in real estate law have stirred as much immediate controversy as Title 5 of the Massachusetts Environmental Code.

Title 5 requires that certain sewage disposal systems be inspected within a period of nine months before or six months after the sale of property, in order to ensure that the systems do not pose a threat to public health and safety or to the environment.

On-site sewage disposal systems include:

- cesspools (a pipe running from a structure and emptying into a single pit) and

- septic systems (a disposal process including a septic tank, distribution box and soil absorption system designed to filter waste and avoid concentrations in the soil).

Approximately 650,000 homes in Massachusetts have on-site systems covered by Title 5.

Systems that show signs of failure or that threaten the environment or public health must be upgraded. However, the Department of Environmental Protection does not require all disposal systems to be in absolute compliance with the rules: "maximum feasible compliance" is the standard that must be met. Alternative technologies (such as sand filters and composting toilets) have been approved. A loan program is available to assist low- and moderate-income homeowners who must upgrade their systems.

The inspection requirement does not apply to any property transfer in which no new parties are involved, such as refinancing, or to transfers by inheritance.

It is generally the owner's responsibility to have his or her system inspected, although the parties may reallocate responsibility by contract. The person acquiring title must be given a copy of the inspection report if inspection occurs prior to the sale. The inspection may be undertaken by an engineer, sanitarian, health officer, home inspector, septage hauler, or other person certified by the Department of Environmental Protection.

Because it is a relatively recent law, the extent of Title 5's practical impact on real estate transactions is still in question, although it has clearly resulted in some degree of confusion in many home sales. Tax credits may be available to offset homeowners' compliance expenses, and some non-complying but non-polluting septic systems may not require replacement.

Title 5 disclosure forms are illustrated in Figures A.4 and A.5.

Figure A.1   Oil and Hazardous Material Inspection Contingency Addendum

INSPECTION CONTINGENCY ADDENDUM (OFFER)
Oil and Hazardous Material

The BUYER may at his own expense and on or before _____, 19_____, have the property professionally inspected for the presence of oil or hazardous material (as such terms are defined in the Massachusetts Oil and Hazardous Material Release Prevention and Response Act, General Laws Chapter 21E). If it is the opinion of such inspector that any such substance is present on the property or that there is a substantial likelihood of a release of any such substance from or at the property, then the BUYER shall have the option of revoking the Offer by written notice to the SELLER and/or the Broker, as the SELLER's agent, prior to the expiration of such time, which notice shall be accompanied by a copy of the inspector's opinion and any related inspection report, whereupon all deposits made by the BUYER to the SELLER shall be forthwith refunded and this Offer shall become null and void and without further recourse to any party.

INITIALS:

_____   _____
Seller (or spouse)   Seller

_____   _____
Buyer   Buyer

_____
Broker(s)

Source: This form has been made available through the courtesy of the Greater Boston Real Estate Board, and is protected by the copyright laws.

Figure A.2   Lead Paint Contingency Addendum

LEAD PAINT CONTINGENCY ADDENDUM (OFFER)

The BUYER may, at the BUYER's own expense and within ten (10) days after the acceptance of this Offer, have the property professionally inspected for the presence of paint, plaster or other accessible materials containing dangerous levels of lead (as such terms are defined by applicable Massachusetts laws and regulations). A copy of the inspector's report shall be furnished to the SELLER upon receipt by the BUYER. If it is the opinion of such inspector that any such materials are present on the property, then the BUYER shall have the option of revoking this Offer by written notice to the SELLER and/or the Broker(s), as agent(s) for the SELLER, prior to the expiration of such time, whereupon all deposits made by the BUYER shall be forthwith refunded and this Offer shall become null and void and without further recourse to either party.

INITIALS:

_____   _____
Seller (or spouse)   Seller

_____   _____
Buyer   Buyer

_____
Broker(s)

Source: This form has been made available through the courtesy of the Greater Boston Real Estate Board, and is protected by the copyright laws.

Figure A.3   Statutory Form of UFFI Disclosure

UFFI DISCLOSURE

The dwelling located at _____
(Number and Street)

_____ , Massachusetts _____
  (City/Town)   *(Zip Code)*

contains urea formaldehyde foam insulation (UFFI). The Commonwealth of Massachusetts has established a program to promote a healthier living environment by identifying the presence of formaldehyde emissions from UFFI in residential dwellings and by facilitating the removal of UFFI from those dwellings where either the formaldehyde level in the air is greater than 0.10 parts per million (ppm), or where an occupant of the dwelling has suffered adverse health effects from the presence of UFFI. Any seller or landlord of a residential dwelling containing UFFI has an affirmative obligation to determine the presence of UFFI and to disclose both its presence and the formaldehyde levels in the dwelling to buyers, tenants or prospective tenants.

UFFI is located in this dwelling in the following places (where checked):

_____ exterior walls: _____
_____ interior walls: _____
_____ floor/ceiling space: _____
_____ attic
_____ other: _____

The date that the UFFI was installed is _____

The air in this dwelling has been tested in accordance with procedures established by the Massachusetts Department of Public Health. A copy of the laboratory report is attached. The test results were as follows:

Location/Room	Formaldehyde level (in parts per million)
_____	_____
_____	_____

By law, no real estate agent, broker or salesperson, and no bank, lending institution or mortgagee doing business in Massachusetts may discriminate in any manner against a dwelling in Massachusetts containing UFFI, or against its owner, when the formaldehyde level in the air of the dwelling is 0.10 ppm or below. I/We attest that all the information provided by me/us in this Disclosure is true and accurate to the best of my/our knowledge.

Date: _____   Signature of Seller(s) or Landlord:

                                      _____

                                      _____

FOR BUYER(S): I/We received this UFFI Disclosure and accompanying current UFFI Information Sheet before giving a deposit on, or signing an Offer to Purchase or a Purchase and Sale Agreement for the dwelling referred to in this Disclosure.

Date: _____   Signature of Buyer(s)

                                      _____

                                      _____

FOR PROSPECTIVE TENANT(S): I/We received this UFFI Disclosure and accompanying UFFI Information sheet before entering into a lease or rental agreement for the dwelling referred to in this Disclosure.

Date: _____   Signature of Prospective Tenant(s)

                                      _____

                                      _____

Figure A.4   Optional Title 5 Disclosure Form

TITLE 5 DISCLOSURE

The Massachusetts Department of Environmental Protection has revised Title 5 of the   State Environmental Code, which regulates on-site, subsurface sewage disposal systems. Effective March 31, 1995, the revised regulations require that the septic system, cesspool or other subsurface sewage disposal system which serves this property be inspected at or within nine months prior to the time of transfer of the title to this property. This requirement, 310 CMR 15.301(1), applies to any transfer of title which occurs on or after March 31, 1995 except for "refinancing or a change in the form of ownership among the same owners, such as placing the facility within a family trust of which the owners are beneficiaries." Local boards of health may adopt more stringent requirements. *A copy of the inspection report must be provided to the buyer or any other person obtaining title to this property.*

310 CMR 15.301(1) further states, "if weather conditions preclude inspection at the time of transfer, the inspection may be completed as soon as weather permits, but in no event later than six months after the transfer provided that the seller notifies the buyer in writing of the requirements of 310 CMR 15.300 through 15.305."

If the system meets one or more failure criteria as stated in 310 CMR 15.303 as documented by an inspection report by an approved System Inspector, the local approving authority, or the Department of Environmental Protection, the system must be upgraded in accordance with the provisions of Title 5.

We, the undersigned, certify that we have read this form in its entirety.

SELLER(S) _____ _____ DATE

BUYER(S) _____ _____ DATE

Figure A.5.   Title 5 Addendum, Offer to Purchase

SEWAGE DISPOSAL SYSTEM CONTINGENCY ADDENDUM
(Offer to Purchase)

The property is serviced by an on-site subsurface sewage disposal system (the "System") regulated by Title 5 of the Massachusetts State Environmental Code ("Title 5"). As required by Title 5, the SELLER will make arrangements to have the System inspected at the SELLER's expense by a person authorized to perform such inspections (the "System Inspector"). The condition of the property shall not be deemed to violate the terms of this Offer because the SELLER is not reasonably able, before the time of the delivery of the deed, to restore any landscaped areas affected by such inspection. Unless, on or before _____, 199__, the SELLER furnishes to the BUYER a certification from the System Inspector, in the form prescribed by the Massachusetts Department of Environmental Protection, stating that the System Inspector has not found any information which indicates that the System fails to adequately protect public health or the environment as defined in Title 5, the BUYER shall have the option of revoking this Offer by written notice to the SELLER and/or the Broker(s), as agent(s) for the SELLER, on or before _____, 199__. If the BUYER so elects to revoke this Offer, all deposits made by the BUYER shall be forthwith refunded and this Offer shall become null and void without further recourse to either party.

INITIALS:

_____   _____
Seller (or spouse)   Seller

_____   _____
Buyer   Buyer

_____
Broker(s)

Source: This form has been made available through the courtesy of the Greater Boston Real Estate Board, and is protected by the copyright laws.

Figure A.6.   Title 5 Addendum, Purchase and Sale Agreement

SEWAGE DISPOSAL SYSTEM CONTINGENCY ADDENDUM
(Purchase and Sale Agreement)

The premises are serviced by an on-site subsurface sewage disposal system (the "System") regulated by Title V of the Massachusetts State Environmental Code ("Title V"). As required by Title V, the SELLER will make arrangements to have the System inspected at the SELLER's expense by a person authorized to perform such inspections (the "System Inspector"). The condition of the premises shall not be deemed to violate this agreement because the SELLER is not reasonably able, before the time of the delivery of the deed, to restore any landscaped areas affected by such inspection. Unless, on or before _____, 199__, the SELLER furnishes to the BUYER a certification from the System Inspector, in the form prescribed by the Massachusetts Department of Environmental Protection, stating that the System Inspector has not found any information which indicates that the System fails to adequately protect public health or the environment as defined in Title V, the BUYER shall have the option of terminating this agreement by written notice to the SELLER and/or the Broker(s), as agent(s) for the SELLER, on or before _____, 199__. If the BUYER so elects to terminate this agreement, any payments made hereunder shall be forthwith refunded and all other obligations of the parties hereto shall cease and this agreement shall be void without recourse to the parties hereto.

INITIALS:

_____   _____
Seller (or spouse)   Seller

_____   _____
Buyer   Buyer

_____
Broker(s)

Source: This form has been made available through the courtesy of the Greater Boston Real Estate Board, and is protected by the copyright laws.

Answer Key

The numbers in parentheses following each answer refer to the page in this Supplement *on which the correct answer is explained.*

Chapter 4

1. d (1)
2. a (1)
3. c (5)
4. a (5)
5. a (4)
6. d (4)
7. b (2)
8. b (3)
9. c (7)
10. c (4)

Chapter 5

1. a (12)
2. b (13)
3. b (13)
4. b (12)
5. c (13)
6. d (12)
7. c (13)
8. d (13)
9. b (13)
10. c (13)

Chapter 6

1. c (19)
2. b (19)
3. d (19)
4. d (19)
5. d (20)
6. a (20)
7. b (21)
8. a (21)
9. d (21)
10. d (22)
11. c (19)
12. a (22)

Chapter 7

1. c (24)
2. d (24)
3. d (25)
4. a (24)
5. d (24)
6. c (24)
7. a (25)
8. c (25)
9. b (25)
10. a (25)

Chapter 8

1. a (27)
2. a (27)
3. c (27)
4. c (28)
5. c (28)
6. c (28)
7. d (28)
8. c (28)
9. c (28)
10. b (28)

Chapter 9

1. a (30)
2. c (30)
3. d (30)
4. c (30)
5. a (30)
6. a (30)
7. d (31)
8. c (31)
9. c (31)
10. a (31)

Chapter 10

1. a (33)
2. a (33)
3. d (33)
4. d (33)
5. c (33)
6. d (33)
7. b (33)
8. d (33)
9. b (34)
10. c (34)

Chapter 11

1. d (48)
2. a (48)
3. c (46)
4. a (46)
5. d (46)
6. a (47)
7. c (47)
8. a (47)
9. c (46)
10. c (46)
11. b (46)
12. b (47)
13. c (49)
14. d (49)
15. b (49)
16. d (49)

Chapter 12

1. b (52)
2. b (53)
3. a (53)
4. c (53)
5. c (52)

Chapter 13

1. c (55)
2. b (56)
3. a (55)
4. a (57)
5. b (56)
6. c (57)
7. c (57)
8. d (58)
9. c (59)
10. b (59)
11. b (57)
12. c (60)
13. b (61)
14. c (60)
15. d (58)

Chapter 14/15

1. c (65)
2. b (65)
3. d (65)
4. c (65)
5. c (65)
6. d (65)
7. d (65)
8. d (65)

Chapter 16

1. c (67)
2. a (67)
3. a (67)
4. b (67)
5. b (67)
6. c (67)
7. c (68)
8. a (68)
9. a (67)
10. a (68)

11. c (69)
12. d (68)

Chapter 18

1. b (71)
2. a (71)
3. d (71)
4. b (71)
5. b (71)
6. c (72)

Chapter 19/20

1. b (74)
2. c (74)
3. b (74)
4. d (74)
5. a (74)
6. b (74)
7. a (75)
8. a (75)
9. c (75)
10. c (75)

Chapter 21

1. c (77)
2. c (77)
3. d (77)
4. b (78)
5. c (77)
6. a (78)
7. a (78)
8. b (78)
9. a (79)
10. b (79)

Index

Abstract, 53
Acceleration clause, 65
Acceptance, 47
Acknowledgment, 46
Addendums, 85-86
  Title 5, 89-90
Adverse possession, 20, 47
Advertising
    apartment service, 60
    bait and switch, 5
    blind, 59
    consumer protection, 5
    discrimination in, 59
Age discrimination, 78
Agency
    disclosure of, 4, 8, 60
    forms of, 4
    law of, 4
    termination of, 7
Antidiscrimination laws, 77-79
Anti-snob zoning, 75
Apartment listing services, 60-61
Appraiser, 13
    certification, 71-72
    general, 71
    license, 71-72
    residential, 71
    trainee, 71, 72
Assessment, 30, 31
Association, license for, 56
Attachment, 4
Attorney, 55, 60
Attorney-in-fact, 55

Bait and switch, 5
Benchmark, 28
Blind advertising, 59
Blockbusting, 79
Board of Registration, 55
Boundary markers, 28
Broker
    advertising by, 59
    compensation, 1-4, 57
    complaints against, 58
    cooperating, 6-7, 12-13
    definition of, 1
    disclosures by, 5-6
    employment, 1
    liability of, 5
    license, 56-58
    monies, 33, 58, 59
    place of business, 57

project, 25
property interest, 59-60
relationships
    buyer, 4
    consumers, 5-7
    disclosure, 60
    fiduciary, 4
    salesperson, 1, 58-59
    seller, 4
Brokerage
    agreement, 1, 9
    business, 1-4
Building codes, 75
Buyer
    brokerage agreement, 9
    default of, 2
    disclosures to, 5-7
    ready, willing, able, 2
    sales contract, 1-2
    title search, 53
Buyer's agent, 4

Certificate
    land court, 52-53
    municipal lien, 30-31
    of title, 53
Cesspools, 84
Clean Waters Act, 82
COALD, 4
Coastal Zone Mgmnt Act, 82
Co-broker agreement, 12-13
Commingling, 58, 68
Commission, 1, 57
    attachment for, 4
    conditions of, 2
    multiple, 3
Competitive market analysis (CMA), 13
Comprehensive Environmental Response,
Compensation and Liability Act (CERCLA), 81
Comprehensive permit, 75
Condominiums, 25
Confidentiality, 72
Consideration, 46
Consumer protection, 5, 69
Contingency addendums
    hazardous material, 85
    lead paint, 86
Continuing education requirement, 62
Contract
    brokerage, 1, 9
    installment, 34
    listing, 1, 12-17

deed of, 19
        tax stamps, 47
Cooperatives, 25
Corporation, license for, 56
Criminal offense, 58, 72
Curtesy, 19, 48

Deceased person, 48-49
Deceptive practices, 5-7
Deed
        easement by, 20
        quitclaim, 20, 46-47
        recording of, 46
        requirements of, 46
        tax, 30
        warranty, 46
Default
        of borrower, 65
        of buyer, 2
        of seller, 34
Delivery, 46
Descent, 19, 48
Developer, 61
Direct reduction loan, 65
Disclosed dual agent, 4
Disclosure
        agency, 4, 8, 10, 60
        apartment service, 61
        by broker, 5-6
        lead paint, 82, 83
        material fact, 6-7
        property interest, 59-60
Discrimination, 58
        in advertising, 59
        age, 79
        complaints of, 79
        exceptions, 78
        practices, 77-78
        renting/leasing, 69
Dower, 19, 48
Dual agency, 4, 10, 57, 60

Earnest money deposit, 33
Easement, 21
        by deed, 20
        by necessity, 20
        by prescription, 20
Education, 56
Election, right of, 48
Enabling acts, 74
Encumbrances, 20-21
Environment issues, 81-90
Estates, 19-20
Eviction, 67
Excise tax, 47
Exclusive agency, 12, 16

Exclusive listing contract, 3
Exclusive-right-to-sell, 12-15

Fair housing, 69, 77-79
Federal Fair housing Act, 79
Fees, 64
Fee simple estate, 25
Fiduciaries, 55
Fiduciary bank account, 59
Foreclosure, 65
Fraudulent intent, 5
Full legal description, 28

Grantee, 46
Grantor, 46

Handicapped individual, 78
Hazardous waste, 81-84
Homestead right, 19-20, 46
Housing
        fair, 69, 77-79
        low-income, 75
        moderate-income, 75

Incompetence, 72
Inspection
        hazardous waste, 82,85
        lead paint, 82-83, 86
        sewer system, 31, 83-84
Installment contract, 34
Insurance, title, 53
Intestate succession, 48-49
Involuntary alienation, 47-48

Joint tenancy, 24

Lakes, 22
Land
        court certificate, 52-53
        registration of, 52-53
Landlord
        eviction notice, 67
        prohibited actions, 69
        responsibilities, 67-68
        security deposit, 69
Land-use controls
        private, 75
        public, 74-75
Lead-based paint, 82-83
Lease
        breach of, 67
        prohibited acts, 69
        proprietary, 25
        provisions, 67-68
Legal description, 28
Legally competent party, 33

Liability, of broker, 5
License, 21
    application, 56
    exam, *v-viii*, 56-58
    fees, 64
    issuance, 57
    nonresident, 56
    renewal, 57, 72
    requirements, 56, 71-72
    revocation, 57-58, 72
    suspension, 57-58, 72
License law, 7
    administration of, 55
    advertising, 59
    apartment services 60
    disclosure, 59-60
    enforcement of, 58
    exceptions, 55
    licensing, 56-58
    out-of-state property, 61
Liens
    mechanic's, 31
    municipal, 30-31
    priority of, 31
    waste clean up, 81-82
Life estate
    dower and curtesy, 19
    homestead, 19-20
Liquidated damages, 33-34
Listing agreement, 1-2
    definition of, 12
    property price and, 13
    types of, 12-13, 14-17
Littoral rights, 21
Loans, 65

Massachusetts
    Board of Registration of Real Estate
    Brokers and Salesmen, 55
    Consumer Protection Act (MCPA), 5, 69
        application of, 5
        compliance with, 6-7
        disclosure, 5-6
        enforcement of, 5
    Law of Descent, 19
    Lead Law, 82-83
    Real Estate License Law, 7, 55-61
Mechanic's lien, 31
Metes-and-bounds, 28
Minors, 78
Model Time-Share Act, 25
Monument, 28
Mortgage
    conditions of, 65
    default, 65
    types of, 65

Municipal lien, 30-31

Navigable waterway, 22
Negligence, 72
Net listing, 13, 58
Nonconforming use, 74
Non-encroachment lines, 82
Nonresident license, 56
Notice, 52
    eviction, 67
    of foreclosure, 65
    of lien, 31

Oceanfront property, 22
Ocean Sanctuaries Act, 82
Offer to purchase, 35-36, 60
    contingency, 85-86
    Title 5 addendum, 89
Open-end mortgage, 65
Open listing, 12, 17
Ownership
    forms of, 24-25
    interests
        encumbrances, 20-21
        estates in land, 19-20
        riparian rights, 21-22

Paint, lead-based, 82-83
Partnership
    license for, 56
    ownership, 24
Personal property, 25
Planning board, 74-75
Ponds, 22
Power of sale clause, 65
Priority, of liens, 31
Procuring cause, 3
Project broker, 25
Promotional sale, 61
Property
    broker's interest in, 59-60
    deceased person's, 48-49
    description of, 28, 46
    oceanfront, 22
    out-of-state, 58, 61
    ownership
    forms of, 24-25
    interests and, 19-22
    personal, 25
    purchase price of, 46
    real, 22, 61
    selling price of, 13
    tax, 30
    transfer of, 46-48
Proposition 2-1/2, 30
Proprietary lease, 25

Public offering, 25
Puffing, 5
Purchase and sale agreement, 37-44
    Title 5 addendum, 90

Quarter-share unit, 25
Quiet enjoyment, 67-68
Quitclaim deed, 20, 46-47

Real property, 22, 61
Rebate, 57
Recording
    of deed, 46
    of title, 52
Redemption, 30
    of mortgage, 65
Reference description, 28
Registration, of land, 52-53
Restrictions, 75
Revenue stamps, 47
Reverse mortgage, 65
Riparian rights, 21-22

Sales contract, 1-2
    contingencies, 85-86
    earnest money, 33
    equitable title, 33
    liquidated damages, 33-34
    offer to purchase, 35-36
    purchase and sale, 37-44
    Statute of Frauds, 33
    Title 5 addendum, 89-90
Salesperson
    advertising by, 59
    and broker, 1, 58-59
    definition of, 1
    handling of money, 58, 59
    license, 56-58
    property interest of, 59-60
Scenic Rivers Act, 82
Scenic roads, 82
Security dealers, 55
Security deposit, 68
Seller's agent, 4
Septic systems, 84
Sewage disposal system
    disclosure, 84, 88-90
    inspection of, 31, 83-84
Signatures, 33
Society, license for, 56
Statute of Frauds
    contract provisions, 33
    lease provisions, 67
Steering, 79
Streams, 22

Street address, 28
Subdivisions, 74-75
Superfund, 81
Survey, 28

Tax
    bills, 30
    deed, 30
    excise, 47
    property, 30
    sale, 30
    transfer, 47
Tenancy in common, 24
Tenancy by entirety, 24
Tenancy at will, 67
Tenant
    eviction of, 67
    pro-tenant legislation, 69
    quiet enjoyment, 67-68
    security deposit, 68
Time-share, 25
Title
    abstract, 53
    action to quiet, 52
    certificate of, 53
    equitable, 33
    evidence of, 53
    insurance, 53
    land court, 53
    recording of, 52
    registration, 52-53
    search, 53
    transfer of, 46-49
Title 5 disclosure, 84, 88-90
    inspection, 31, 83-84
Title theory, 65
Transfer tax, 47

Uniform Building Code, 75
Uniform Partnership Act, 24
Urea formaldehyde foam insulation, 78, 83, 87

Value, assessed, 30
Variance, 74
Voluntary alienation, 46-47

Warranty deed, 46
Waterway
    navigable, 22
    non-encroachment lines, 82
Wetlands, 81
Wetlands Restriction Act, 82
Will, 48

Zoning, 74-75
    board of appeals, 74